BRITISH R  .3

CW00517478

MULTIPLE UNITS

TWENTY-SECOND EDITION
2009

The complete guide to all Diesel Multiple Units which operate on the National Rail network

UPDATED TO 2011 EDITION 1. 1. 11

Robert Pritchard & Peter Fox

ISBN 978 1902 336 68 8

© 2008. Platform 5 Publishing Ltd., 3 Wyvern House, Sark Road, Sheffield, S2 4HG, England.

CONTENTS

PROVISION OF INFORMATION

This book has been compiled with care to be as accurate as possible, but in some cases information is not officially available and the publisher cannot be held responsible for any errors or omissions. We would like to thank the companies and individuals which have been co-operative in supplying information to us. The authors of this series of books are always pleased to receive notification from readers of any inaccuracies readers may find in the series, to enhance future editions. Please send comments to:

Robert Pritchard, Platform 5 Publishing Ltd., 3 Wyvern House, Sark Road, Sheffield, S2 4HG, England.

Tel: 0114 255 2625   **Fax:** 0114 255 2471
e-mail: robert@platform5.com

This book is updated to 3 October 2008.

UPDATES

This book is updated to the Stock Changes given in **Today's Railways UK 83** (November 2008). Readers are therefore advised to update this book from the official Platform 5 Stock Changes published every month in **Today's Railways UK** magazine, starting with issue 84.

The Platform 5 magazine **Today's Railways UK** contains news and rolling stock information on the railways of Britain and Ireland and is published on the second Monday of every month. For further details of **Today's Railways UK**, please see the advertisement on the back cover of this book.

BRITAIN'S RAILWAY SYSTEM

INFRASTRUCTURE & OPERATION

Britain's national railway infrastructure is owned by a "not for dividend" company, Network Rail. Many stations and maintenance depots are leased to and operated by Train Operating Companies (TOCs), but some larger stations remain under Network Rail control. The only exception is the infrastructure on the Isle of Wight, which is nationally owned and is leased to South West Trains.

Trains are operated by TOCs over Network Rail, regulated by access agreements between the parties involved. In general, TOCs are responsible for the provision and maintenance of the locos, rolling stock and staff necessary for the direct operation of services, whilst NR is responsible for the provision and maintenance of the infrastructure and also for staff to regulate the operation of services.

DOMESTIC PASSENGER TRAIN OPERATORS

The large majority of passenger trains are operated by the TOCs on fixed term franchises. Franchise expiry dates are shown in parentheses in the list of franchisees below:

Franchise	Franchisee	Trading Name
Chiltern Railways	M40 Trains Ltd. (until 1 March 2022)	Chiltern Railways
Cross-Country[1]	Arriva Trains Ltd. (until 1 November 2013)	Cross-Country
East Midlands[2]	Stagecoach Holdings plc (until 11 November 2013)	East Midlands Trains
Greater Western[3]	First Group plc (until 1 April 2013)	First Great Western
Greater Anglia[4]	National Express Group plc (until 1 April 2011)	National Express East Anglia
Integrated Kent[5]	GoVia Ltd. (Go-Ahead/Keolis) (until 3 March 2012)	Southeastern
InterCity East Coast[6]	National Express Group plc (until 9 November 2013)	National Express East Coast
InterCity West Coast	Virgin Rail Group Ltd. (until 31 March 2012)	Virgin Trains
London Rail[7]	MTR/Laing Rail (until 11 November 2014)	London Overground
LTS Rail[8]	National Express Group plc (until 25 May 2011)	c2c
Merseyrail Electrics[9]	Serco/NedRail (until 20 July 2028)	Merseyrail Electrics
Northern Rail[10]	Serco/NedRail (until 12 September 2011)	Northern
ScotRail[11]	First Group plc (until 8 November 2014)	First ScotRail

South Central[12]	GoVia Ltd. (Go-Ahead/Keolis) (until 20 September 2009)	Southern
South Western[13]	Stagecoach Holdings plc (until 4 February 2014)	South West Trains
Thameslink/Great Northern[14]	First Group plc (until 1 April 2012)	First Capital Connect
Trans-Pennine Express[15]	First Group/Keolis (until 1 February 2012)	First Trans-Pennine Express
Wales & Borders	Arriva Trains Ltd. (until 6 December 2018)	Arriva Trains Wales
West Midlands[16]	GoVia Ltd. (Go-Ahead/Keolis) (until 19 September 2013)	London Midland

Notes:

[1] Awarded for six years to 2013 with an extension for a further two years and five months to April 2016 if performance targets are met.

[2] Awarded for six years to 2013 with an extension for a further one year and five months to April 2015 if performance targets are met.

[3] Awarded for seven years to 2013 with an extension for a further three years to April 2016 if performance targets are met.

[4] Awarded for seven years to 2011 with an extension for a further three years to April 2014 if performance targets are met. Franchise was branded "One" from April 2004 to February 2008.

[5] The Integrated Kent franchise started on 1 April 2006 for an initial period of six years to 2012, with an extension for a further two years to April 2014 if performance targets are met.

[6] Awarded for five years and 11 months to 2013 with an extension for a further one year and five months to April 2015 if performance targets are met. National Express took over the new East Coast franchise following the financial difficulties experienced with GNER's holding company Sea Containers.

[7] The London Rail Concession is different from all other rail franchises, as fares and service levels are set by Transport for London instead of the DfT. Incorporates the North and West London lines, the Gospel Oak–Barking line and Euston–Watford local services.

[8] The LTS Rail franchise is due to be rebranded as part of National Express Group's adoption of a new unified identity for all of its operations, but the new brand had not been selected at the time of going to press.

[9] Now under control of Merseytravel PTE instead of the DfT. Franchise due to be reviewed after seven years (in July 2010) and then every five years to fit in with the Merseyside Local Transport Plan.

[10] Awarded for six years and nine months to 2011 with an extension for a further two years to September 2013 if performance targets are met.

[11] The ScotRail franchise was extended for three further years in 2008.

[12] The South Central franchise termination date has been brought forward by three months to ensure that the winner of the new franchise has already taken over before any major timetable changes are made in December 2009.

[13] Awarded for seven years to 2014 with an extension for a further three years to February 2017 if performance targets are met.

[14] Awarded for six years to 2012 with an extension for up to a further three years to April 2015 if performance targets are met.

[15] Awarded for eight years to 2012 with an extension a further five years to February 2017 if performance targets are met.

[16] Awarded for six years to 2013 with an extension for a further two years to September 2015 if performance targets are met.

All new franchises officially start at 02.00 on the first day. Because of this the finishing date of an old franchise and the start date of its successor are the same.

Where termination dates are dependent on performance targets being met, the earliest possible termination date is generally given. However, in the case of Chiltern and Merseyrail, the termination dates are based on the maximum franchise length.

The following operators run non-franchised services only:

Operator	Trading Name	Route
BAA	Heathrow Express	London Paddington–Heathrow Airport
First Hull Trains	First Hull Trains	London King's Cross–Hull
Grand Central	Grand Central	London King's Cross–Sunderland
West Coast Railway Company	West Coast Railway Company	Birmingham–Stratford-upon-Avon Fort William–Mallaig* York–Harrogate–Leeds–York–Scarborough* Machynlleth–Porthmadog/Pwllheli*
Wrexham, Shropshire & Marylebone Railway	Wrexham & Shropshire	London Marylebone–Wrexham General

* Special summer-dated services only.

INTERNATIONAL PASSENGER OPERATIONS

Eurostar (UK) operates passenger services between the UK and mainland Europe, jointly with the national operators of France (SNCF) and Belgium (SNCB/NMBS). Eurostar (UK) is a subsidiary of London & Continental Railways, which is jointly owned by National Express Group and British Airways.

In addition, a service for the conveyance of accompanied road vehicles through the Channel Tunnel is provided by the tunnel operating company, Eurotunnel.

FREIGHT TRAIN OPERATIONS

The following operators operate freight train services under "Open Access" arrangements:

English Welsh & Scottish Railway (EWS)
Freightliner
Direct Rail Services (DRS)
First GBRf

Fastline (Jarvis)
Advenza (Cotswold Rail)
Colas Rail
West Coast Railway Company

INTRODUCTION

DMU CLASSES

DMU Classes are listed in class number order. Principal details and dimensions are quoted for each class in metric and/or imperial units as considered appropriate bearing in mind common usage in the UK.

All dimensions and weights are quoted for vehicles in an "as new" condition with all necessary supplies (e.g. oil, water, sand) on board. Dimensions are quoted in the order Length – Width. All lengths quoted are over buffers or couplers as appropriate. Where two lengths are quoted, the first refers to outer vehicles in a set and the second to inner vehicles. All width dimensions quoted are maxima.

NUMERICAL LISTINGS

DMUs are listed in numerical order of set – using current numbers as allocated by the RSL. Individual "loose" vehicles are listed in numerical order after vehicles formed into fixed formations. Where sets or vehicles have been renumbered in recent years, former numbering detail is shown in parentheses. Each entry is laid out as in the following example:

RSL Set No.	Detail	Livery	Owner	Operator	Depot	Formation		Name
142 073	v	**AV**	A	AW	CF	55723	55769	Myfanwy

Detail Differences. Detail differences which currently affect the areas and types of train which vehicles may work are shown, plus differences in interior layout. Where such differences occur within a class, these are shown either in the heading information or alongside the individual set or vehicle number. The following standard abbreviation is used:

r   Radio Electronic Token Block (RETB) equipment.

In all cases use of the above abbreviation indicates the equipment indicated is normally operable. Meaning of non-standard abbreviations is detailed in individual class headings.

Set Formations. Regular set formations are shown where these are normally maintained. Readers should note set formations might be temporarily varied from time to time to suit maintenance and/or operational requirements. Vehicles shown as "spare" are not formed in any regular set formation.

Codes. Codes are used to denote the livery, owner, operation and depot of each unit. Details of these will be found in section 5 of this book. Where a unit or spare car is off-lease, the operator column will be left blank.

Names. Only names carried with official sanction are listed. As far as possible names are shown in UPPER/lower case characters as actually shown on the name carried on the vehicle(s). Unless otherwise shown, complete units are regarded as named rather than just the individual car(s) which carry the name.

GENERAL INFORMATION

CLASSIFICATION AND NUMBERING

First generation ("Heritage") DMUs are classified in the series 100–139.
Second generation DMUs are classified in the series 140–199.
Diesel-electric multiple units are classified in the series 200–249.
Service units are classified in the series 930–999.
First and second generation individual cars are numbered in the series 50000–59999 and 79000–79999.

DEMU individual cars are numbered in the series 60000–60999, except for a few former EMU vehicles which retain their EMU numbers.

Service stock individual cars are numbered in the series 975000–975999 and 977000–977999, although this series is not exclusively used for DMU vehicles.

OPERATING CODES

These codes are used by train operating company staff to describe the various different types of vehicles and normally appear on data panels on the inner (i.e. non driving) ends of vehicles.

The first part of the code describes whether or not the car has a motor or a driving cab as follows:

DM Driving motor.
M   Motor
DT Driving trailer
T   Trailer

The next letter is a "B" for cars with a brake compartment.

This is followed by the saloon details:

F   First
S   Standard
C   Composite
so denotes a semi-open vehicle (part compartments, part open). All other vehicles are assumed to consist solely of open saloons.

L denotes a vehicle with a toilet.

Finally vehicles with a buffet are suffixed RB or RMB for a miniature buffet.

Where two vehicles of the same type are formed within the same unit, the above codes may be suffixed by (A) and (B) to differentiate between the vehicles.

A composite is a vehicle containing both first and standard class accommodation, whilst a brake vehicle is a vehicle containing separate specific accommodation for the conductor.

Special Note: Where vehicles have been declassified, the correct operating code which describes the actual vehicle layout is quoted in this publication.

BUILD DETAILS

Lot Numbers

Vehicles ordered under the auspices of BR were allocated a Lot (batch) number when ordered and these are quoted in class headings and sub-headings.

BUILDERS

These are shown in class headings. The workshops of British Railways and the pre-nationalisation and pre-grouping companies were first transferred to a wholly-owned subsidiary called "British Rail Engineering Ltd.", abbreviated to BREL. These workshops were later privatised, BREL then becoming "BREL Ltd.". Some of the works were then taken over by ABB, which was later merged with Daimler-Benz Transportation to become "Adtranz". This company has now been taken over by Bombardier Transportation, which had taken over Procor at Horbury previously. Bombardier also builds vehicles for the British market in Brugge, Belgium.

Other workshops were the subject of separate sales, Springburn, Glasgow and Wolverton becoming "Railcare" and Eastleigh becoming "Wessex Traincare". These then became owned by Alstom (previously GEC-Alsthom), as did the former Metro-Cammell Works in Birmingham (now closed). Springburn and Wolverton are now again owned by Railcare, whilst Eastleigh Works is now operated by Knights Rail Services and Wabtec.

Note: Part of Doncaster works was sold to RFS Engineering, which became insolvent and was bought out and renamed RFS Industries. This has now been taken over by Wabtec.

The builder details in the class headings show the owner at the time of vehicle construction followed by the works as follows:

Birmingham	The former Metro-Cammell works at Saltley, Birmingham.
Derby	Derby Carriage Works (also known as Litchurch Lane).
Eastleigh	Eastleigh Works.
Wakefield	Horbury Works.
York	York Carriage Works.

Other builders are:

Alexander	Walter Alexander, Falkirk.
Barclay	Andrew Barclay, Caledonia Works, Kilmarnock (now Brush-Barclay).
Gloucester	Gloucester Railway Carriage & Wagon, Gloucester.
Leyland Bus	Leyland Bus, Workington.
Metro-Cammell	Metropolitan-Cammell, Saltley, Birmingham
Pressed Steel	Pressed Steel, Linwood.
Siemens	Siemens Transportation Systems (various works in Germany, Austria and the Czech Republic, principally Uerdinden (Krefeld), Germany, Wien (Vienna), Austria and Praha (Prague), Czech Republic.

ACCOMMODATION

The information given in class headings and sub-headings is in the form F/S nT (or TD) nW. For example 12/54 1T 1W denotes 12 first class and 54 standard class seats, one toilet and one space for a wheelchair. A number in brackets (i.e. (2)) denotes tip-up seats (in addition to the fixed seats). Tip-up seats in vestibules do not count. The seating layout of open saloons is shown as 2+1, 2+2 or 3+2 as the case may be. Where units have first class accommodation as well as standard and the layout is different for each class then these are shown separately prefixed by "1:" and "2:". TD denotes a toilet suitable for use by a disabled person.

ABBREVIATIONS

The following abbreviations are used in class headings and also throughout this publication:

BR	British Railways.
BSI	Bergische Stahl Industrie.
DEMU	Diesel Electric Multiple Unit.
DMU	Diesel Multiple Unit (general term).
EMU	Electric Multiple Unit.
kN	kilonewtons.
km/h	kilometres per hour.
kW	kilowatts.
LT	London Transport.
LUL	London Underground Limited.
m.	metres.
m.p.h.	miles per hour.
t.	tonnes.

1. DIESEL MECHANICAL & DIESEL HYDRAULIC UNITS

FIRST GENERATION UNITS

CLASS 121   PRESSED STEEL SUBURBAN

First generation units used by Chiltern Railways on selected Aylesbury–Princes Risborough services (121 020) and by Arriva Trains Wales on Cardiff Queen Street–Cardiff Bay shuttles (121 032).

Construction: Steel.
Engines: Two Leyland 1595 of 112 kW (150 h.p.) at 1800 r.p.m.
Transmission: Mechanical. Cardan shaft and freewheel to a four-speed epicyclic gearbox and final drive.
Bogies: DD10.
Brakes: Vacuum.
Couplers: Screw.
Dimensions: 20.45 x 2.82 m.
Gangways: Non gangwayed single cars with cabs at each end.
Wheel arrangement: 1-A + A-1.
Doors: Manually-operated slam.
Maximum Speed: 70 m.p.h.
Seating Layout: 3+2 facing.
Multiple Working: "Blue Square" coupling code. First Generation vehicles cannot be coupled to Second Generation units.

55020/55032. DMBS. Lot No. 30518 1960/1961. –/65. 38.0 t.

Non-standard livery: 121 020 All over Chiltern blue with a silver stripe.

Notes: Fitted with central door locking.

121 020 formerly in departmental use as unit 960 002 (977722).

121 032 formerly in departmental use as 977842, and more recently in preservation at The Railway Age, Crewe.

| 121 020 | **0** | CR | *CR* | AL | 55020 |
| 121 032 | **AV** | AW | *AW* | CF | 55032 |

PARRY PEOPLE MOVERS

CLASS 139   PPM-60

Gas/flywheel hybrid drive Railcars on order for use on the Stourbridge Junction to Stourbridge Town branch from December 2008.
Body construction: Stainless steel framework.
Chassis construction: Welded mild steel box section.
Primary Drive: Ford MVH420 2.0 litre LPG fuel engine driving through Newage marine gearbox, Tandler bevel box and 4 "V" belt driver to flywheel.
Flywheel Energy Store: 500 kg, 1 m diameter, normal operational speed range 1000–1500 r.p.m.
Final transmission: 4 "V" belt driver from flywheel to Tandler bevel box, Linde hydrostatic transmission and spiral bevel gearbox at No. 2 end axle.
Braking: Normal service braking by regeneration to flywheel (1 m/s/s); emergency/parking braking by sprung-on, air-off disc brakes (3 m/s/s).
Maximum Speed: 40 m.p.h.
Dimensions: 8.7 x 2.4 m.
Doors: Deans powered doors, double-leaf folding (one per side).
Seating Layout:
Multiple Working: Not applicable.

39001–39002. DMS. Main Road Sheet Metal, Leyland 2007–08. –/   1W.   . t.

139 001	**LM**	P		39001
139 002	**LM**	P		39002

SECOND GENERATION UNITS

All units in this section have air brakes and are equipped with public address, with transmission equipment on driving vehicles and flexible diaphragm gangways. Except where otherwise stated, transmission is Voith 211r hydraulic with a cardan shaft to a Gmeinder GM190 final drive.

CLASS 142   PACER   BREL DERBY/LEYLAND

DMS–DMSL.

Construction: Steel underframe, aluminium alloy body and roof. Built from Leyland National bus parts on four-wheeled underframes.
Engines: One Cummins LTA10-R of 172 kW (230 h.p.) at 2100 r.p.m.
Couplers: BSI at outer ends, bar within unit.
Dimensions: 15.45 x 2.80 m.
Gangways: Within unit only.   **Wheel Arrangement:** 1-A + A-1.
Doors: Twin-leaf inward pivoting.   **Maximum Speed:** 75 m.p.h.
Seating Layout: 3+2 mainly unidirectional bus/bench style unless stated.
Multiple Working: Within class and with Classes 143, 144, 150, 153, 155, 156, 158 and 159.

55542–55591. DMS. Lot No. 31003 1985–1986. –/62 (c –/46(6) 2W, s –/56, t –/53 or 55 1W, u –/52 or 54 1W). 24.5 t.
55592–55641. DMSL. Lot No. 31004 1985–1986. –/59 1T (c –/44(6) 1T 2W, s –/50 1T, u –/60 1T). 25.0 t.
55701–55746. DMS. Lot No. 31013 1986–1987. –/62 (c –/46(6) 2W, s –/56, t –/53 or 55 1W, u –/52 or 54 1W). 24.5 t.
55747–55792. DMSL. Lot No. 31014 1986–1987. –/59 1T (c –/44(6) 1T 2W, s –/50 1T, u –/60 1T). 25.0 t.

Notes:

c   Refurbished Arriva Trains Wales units. Fitted with 2+2 individual Chapman seating.
s   Fitted with 2+2 individual high-back seating.
t   Former First North Western facelifted units – DMS fitted with a luggage/bicycle rack and wheelchair space.
u   Merseytravel units – Fitted with 3+2 individual low-back seating.

The following units are on sub-lease from Northern to First Great Western until early December 2008: 142 004/028/062/067/070.
The following units are on sub-lease from Northern to First Great Western until 30 June 2010: 142 001/009/029/030/063/064/068.

142 001	t	**NW**	A	*GW*	EX	55542	55592
142 002	c	**AV**	A	*AW*	CF	55543	55593
142 003		**NO**	A	*NO*	NH	55544	55594
142 004	t	**NW**	A	*GW*	EX	55545	55595
142 005	t	**NO**	A	*NO*	NH	55546	55596
142 006	c	**AV**	A	*AW*	CF	55547	55597
142 007	t	**NO**	A	*NO*	NH	55548	55598
142 009	t	**NW**	A	*GW*	EX	55550	55600
142 010	c	**AV**	A	*AW*	CF	55551	55601
142 011	t	**NO**	A	*NO*	NH	55552	55602
142 012	t	**NO**	A	*NO*	NH	55553	55603
142 013		**NO**	A	*NO*	NH	55554	55604
142 014	t	**NO**	A	*NO*	NH	55555	55605
142 015	s	**AV**	A	*NO*	HT	55556	55606
142 016	s	**AV**	A	*NO*	HT	55557	55607
142 017	s	**AV**	A	*NO*	HT	55558	55608
142 018	s	**AV**	A	*NO*	HT	55559	55609
142 019	s	**NO**	A	*NO*	HT	55560	55610
142 020	s	**NO**	A	*NO*	HT	55561	55611
142 021	s	**NO**	A	*NO*	HT	55562	55612
142 022	s	**AV**	A	*NO*	HT	55563	55613
142 023	t	**NO**	A	*NO*	HT	55564	55614
142 024	s	**NO**	A	*NO*	HT	55565	55615
142 025	s	**NO**	A	*NO*	HT	55566	55616
142 026	s	**NO**	A	*NO*	HT	55567	55617
142 027	t	**NO**	A	*NO*	HT	55568	55618
142 028	t	**NW**	A	*GW*	EX	55569	55619
142 029		**NW**	A	*GW*	EX	55570	55620
142 030		**NW**	A	*GW*	EX	55571	55621
142 031	t	**NO**	A	*NO*	NH	55572	55622

142 032	t	**NO**	A	*NO*	NH	55573	55623	
142 033	t	**NO**	A	*NO*	NH	55574	55624	
142 034	t	**NO**	A	*NO*	NH	55575	55625	
142 035	t	**NO**	A	*NO*	NH	55576	55626	
142 036	t	**NO**	A	*NO*	NH	55577	55627	
142 037	t	**NO**	A	*NO*	NH	55578	55628	
142 038	t	**NO**	A	*NO*	NH	55579	55629	
142 039	t	**NO**	A	*NO*	NH	55580	55630	
142 040	t	**NO**	A	*NO*	NH	55581	55631	
142 041	u	**NO**	A	*NO*	NH	55582	55632	
142 042	u	**NO**	A	*NO*	NH	55583	55633	
142 043	u	**NO**	A	*NO*	NH	55584	55634	
142 044	u	**NO**	A	*NO*	NH	55585	55635	
142 045	u	**NO**	A	*NO*	NH	55586	55636	
142 046	u	**NO**	A	*NO*	NH	55587	55637	
142 047	u	**NO**	A	*NO*	NH	55588	55638	
142 048	u	**NO**	A	*NO*	NH	55589	55639	
142 049	u	**NO**	A	*NO*	NH	55590	55640	
142 050	s	**NO**	A	*NO*	HT	55591	55641	
142 051	u	**NO**	A	*NO*	NH	55701	55747	
142 052	u	**NO**	A	*NO*	NH	55702	55748	
142 053	u	**NO**	A	*NO*	NH	55703	55749	
142 054	u	**MY**	A	*NO*	NH	55704	55750	
142 055	u	**MY**	A	*NO*	NH	55705	55751	
142 056	u	**MY**	A	*NO*	NH	55706	55752	
142 057	u	**MY**	A	*NO*	NH	55707	55753	
142 058	u	**MY**	A	*NO*	NH	55708	55754	
142 060	t	**NO**	A	*NO*	NH	55710	55756	
142 061	t	**NO**	A	*NO*	NH	55711	55757	
142 062	t	**NW**	A	*GW*	EX	55712	55758	
142 063	t	**NW**	A	*GW*	EX	55713	55759	
142 064	t	**NW**	A	*GW*	EX	55714	55760	
142 065	s	**NO**	A	*NO*	HT	55715	55761	
142 066	s	**NO**	A	*NO*	HT	55716	55762	
142 067		**NW**	A	*GW*	EX	55717	55763	
142 068	t	**NW**	A	*GW*	EX	55718	55764	
142 069	c	**AV**	A	*AW*	CF	55719	55765	
142 070	t	**NW**	A	*GW*	EX	55720	55766	
142 071	s	**AV**	A		HT	55721	55767	
142 072	c	**AV**	A	*AW*	CF	55722	55768	
142 073	c	**AV**	A	*AW*	CF	55723	55769	Myfanwy
142 074	c	**AV**	A	*AW*	CF	55724	55770	
142 075	c	**AV**	A	*AW*	CF	55725	55771	
142 076	c	**AV**	A	*AW*	CF	55726	55772	
142 077	c	**AV**	A	*AW*	CF	55727	55773	
142 078	s	**AV**	A	*NO*	HT	55728	55774	
142 079	s	**AV**	A	*NO*	HT	55729	55775	
142 080	c	**AV**	A	*AW*	CF	55730	55776	
142 081	c	**AV**	A	*AW*	CF	55731	55777	
142 082	c	**AV**	A	*AW*	CF	55732	55778	
142 083	c	**AV**	A	*AW*	CF	55733	55779	

142 084	s	**NO**	A	*NO*	HT	55734 55780
142 085	c	**AV**	A	*AW*	CF	55735 55781
142 086	s	**NO**	A	*NO*	HT	55736 55782
142 087	s	**AV**	A	*NO*	HT	55737 55783
142 088	s	**AV**	A	*NO*	HT	55738 55784
142 089	s	**NO**	A	*NO*	HT	55739 55785
142 090	s	**AV**	A	*NO*	HT	55740 55786
142 091	s	**AV**	A	*NO*	HT	55741 55787
142 092	s	**AV**	A	*NO*	HT	55742 55788
142 093	s	**AV**	A	*NO*	HT	55743 55789
142 094	s	**AV**	A	*NO*	HT	55744 55790
142 095	s	**AV**	A	*NO*	HT	55745 55791
142 096	s	**AV**	A	*NO*	HT	55746 55792

CLASS 143   PACER   ALEXANDER/BARCLAY

DMS–DMSL. Similar design to Class 142, but bodies built by W. Alexander with Barclay underframes.

Construction: Steel underframe, aluminium alloy body and roof. Alexander bus bodywork on four-wheeled underframes.
Engines: One Cummins LTA10-R of 172 kW (230 h.p.) at 2100 r.p.m.
Couplers: BSI at outer ends, bar within unit.
Dimensions: 15.45 x 2.80 m.
Gangways: Within unit only.   **Wheel Arrangement:** 1-A + A-1.
Doors: Twin-leaf inward pivoting.   **Maximum Speed:** 75 m.p.h.
Seating Layout: 2+2 high-back Chapman seating, mainly unidirectional.
Multiple Working: Within class and with Classes 142, 144, 150, 153, 155, 156, 158 and 159.

DMS. Lot No. 31005 Andrew Barclay 1985–1986. –/48(6) 2W. 24.0 t.
DMSL. Lot No. 31006 Andrew Barclay 1985–1986. –/44(6) 1T 2W. 24.5 t.

143 601	**AV**	BC	*AW*	CF	55642 55667	
143 602	**AV**	P	*AW*	CF	55651 55668	
143 603	**FI**	P	*GW*	PM	55658 55669	
143 604	**AV**	P	*AW*	CF	55645 55670	
143 605	**AV**	P	*AW*	CF	55646 55671	
143 606	**AV**	P	*AW*	CF	55647 55672	
143 607	**AV**	P	*AW*	CF	55648 55673	
143 608	**AV**	P	*AW*	CF	55649 55674	
143 609	**AV**	CC	*AW*	CF	55650 55675	Sir Tom Jones
143 610	**AV**	BC	*AW*	CF	55643 55676	
143 611	**BI**	P	*GW*	PM	55652 55677	
143 612	**BI**	P	*GW*	PM	55653 55678	
143 614	**AV**	BC	*AW*	CF	55655 55680	
143 616	**AV**	P	*AW*	CF	55657 55682	
143 617	**FI**	RI	*GW*	PM	55644 55683	
143 618	**BI**	RI	*GW*	PM	55659 55684	
143 619	**BI**	RI	*GW*	PM	55660 55685	
143 620	**BI**	P	*GW*	PM	55661 55686	
143 621	**BI**	P	*GW*	PM	55662 55687	

143 622	**AV**	P	*AW*	CF	55663	55688
143 623	**AV**	P	*AW*	CF	55664	55689
143 624	**AV**	P	*AW*	CF	55665	55690
143 625	**AV**	P	*AW*	CF	55666	55691

CLASS 144 PACER ALEXANDER/BREL DERBY

DMS–DMSL or DMS–MS–DMSL. As Class 143, but underframes built by BREL.

Construction: Steel underframe, aluminium alloy body and roof. Alexander bus bodywork on four-wheeled underframes.
Engines: One Cummins LTA10-R of 172 kW (230 h.p.) at 2100 r.p.m.
Couplers: BSI at outer ends, bar within unit.
Dimensions: 15.45/15.43 x 2.80 m.

Gangways: Within unit only.	**Wheel Arrangement:** 1-A + A-1.
Doors: Twin-leaf inward pivoting.	**Maximum Speed:** 75 m.p.h.

Seating Layout: 2+2 high-back Richmond seating, mainly unidirectional.
Multiple Working: Within class and with Classes 142, 143, 150, 153, 155, 156, 158 and 159.

DMS. Lot No. 31015 BREL Derby 1986–1987. –/45(3) 1W 24.0 t.
MS. Lot No. BREL Derby 31037 1987. –/58. 23.5 t.
DMSL. Lot No. BREL Derby 31016 1986–1987. –/42(3) 1T. 24.5 t.

Note: The centre cars of the 3-car units are owned by West Yorkshire PTE, although managed by Porterbrook Leasing Company.

144 001	**YP**	P	*NO*	NL	55801		55824
144 002	**YP**	P	*NO*	NL	55802		55825
144 003	**YP**	P	*NO*	NL	55803		55826
144 004	**YP**	P	*NO*	NL	55804		55827
144 005	**YP**	P	*NO*	NL	55805		55828
144 006	**YP**	P	*NO*	NL	55806		55829
144 007	**YP**	P	*NO*	NL	55807		55830
144 008	**YP**	P	*NO*	NL	55808		55831
144 009	**YP**	P	*NO*	NL	55809		55832
144 010	**YP**	P	*NO*	NL	55810		55833
144 011	**YP**	P	*NO*	NL	55811		55834
144 012	**YP**	P	*NO*	NL	55812		55835
144 013	**YP**	P	*NO*	NL	55813		55836
144 014	**YP**	P	*NO*	NL	55814	55850	55837
144 015	**YP**	P	*NO*	NL	55815	55851	55838
144 016	**YP**	P	*NO*	NL	55816	55852	55839
144 017	**YP**	P	*NO*	NL	55817	55853	55840
144 018	**YP**	P	*NO*	NL	55818	55854	55841
144 019	**YP**	P	*NO*	NL	55819	55855	55842
144 020	**YP**	P	*NO*	NL	55820	55856	55843
144 021	**YP**	P	*NO*	NL	55821	55857	55844
144 022	**YP**	P	*NO*	NL	55822	55858	55845
144 023	**YP**	P	*NO*	NL	55823	55859	55846

Name (carried on DMSL):

144 001 THE PENISTONE LINE PARTNERSHIP

CLASS 150/0   SPRINTER   BREL YORK

DMSL–MS–DMS. Prototype Sprinter.

Construction: Steel.
Engines: One Cummins NT-855-R4 of 213 kW (285 h.p.) at 2100 r.p.m.
Bogies: BX8P (powered), BX8T (non-powered).
Couplers: BSI at outer end of driving vehicles, bar non-driving ends.
Dimensions: 20.06/20.18 x 2.82 m.
Gangways: Within unit only.   **Wheel Arrangement:** 2-B + 2-B + B-2.
Doors: Twin-leaf sliding.   **Maximum Speed:** 75 m.p.h.
Seating Layout: 3+2 (mainly unidirectional).
Multiple Working: Within class and with Classes 142, 143, 144, 153, 155, 156, 158, 159, 170 and 172.

DMSL. Lot No. 30984 1984. –/72 1T. 35.4 t.
MS. Lot No. 30986 1984. –/92. 34.1 t.
DMS. Lot No. 30985 1984. –/76. 29.5 t.

150 001		**CI**	A	*LM*	TS	55200	55400	55300
150 002		**CI**	A	*LM*	TS	55201	55401	55301

CLASS 150/1   SPRINTER   BREL YORK

DMSL–DMS or DMSL–DMSL–DMS or DMSL–DMS–DMS.

Construction: Steel.
Engines: One Cummins NT855R5 of 213 kW (285 h.p.) at 2100 r.p.m.
Bogies: BP38 (powered), BT38 (non-powered).
Couplers: BSI.
Dimensions: 19.74 x 2.82 m.
Gangways: Within unit only.   **Wheel Arrangement:** 2-B (+ 2–B) + B-2.
Doors: Twin-leaf sliding.   **Maximum Speed:** 75 m.p.h.
Seating Layout: 3+2 facing as built but Centro units were reseated with mainly unidirectional seating.
Multiple Working: Within class and with Classes 142, 143, 144, 153, 155, 156, 158, 159, 170 and 172.

DMSL. Lot No. 31011 1985–1986. –/72 1T (c –/59 1TD (except 52144 which is –/62 1TD), t –/71 1T, u –/71 1T). 38.3 t.
DMS. Lot No. 31012 1985–1986. –/76 (c –/65, t –/73, u –/70). 38.1 t.

Northern promotional vinyls: 150 146 & 150 147 Liverpool: European Capital of Culture.

Notes: The centre cars of 3-car units are Class 150/2 vehicles. For details see Class 150/2.

c   3+2 Chapman seating.

150 003	u	**WM**	A	*LM*	TS	52103	57210	57103
150 005	u	**CI**	A	*LM*	TS	52105	52210	57105
150 007	u	**CI**	A	*LM*	TS	52107	52202	57107
150 009	u	**CI**	A	*LM*	TS	52109	57202	57109

▲ The first completed bodyshell of two Parry People Movers for London Midland, numbered 139 001, was displayed on a low loader at Tyseley on 28/06/08. These will enter service on the Stourbridge branch from December 2008. **Robert Pritchard**

▼ Arriva Trains-liveried 142 072 and 143 610 pass Cardiff Queen Street North Junction with the 15.17 Bargoed–Penarth on 17/10/07. **Andrew Mist**

▲ 143 616 and 143 601 arrive at Radyr with the 12.39 Pontypridd–Cardiff Central on 06/08/07. **John Binch**

▼ 3-car Class 144 No. 144 020, in West Yorkshire PTE-livery, arrives at Sheffield on 26/09/07 forming the 14.34 from Leeds via Barnsley. **Peter Fox**

First Group "Dynamic Lines"-liveried 150 261 pauses at Saltash with the 17.06 Plymouth–Liskeard on 09/06/08.
Robert Pritchard

Arriva Trains-liveried 150 259 and 150 227 are seen south of Cwm on the newly reopened Ebbw Vale branch with the 13.40 Ebbw Vale Parkway–Cardiff Central on 18/02/08. **Andrew Mist**

▲ Northern-liveried 153 316 waits departure from Sheffield with the 10.44 to Gainsborough Lea Road on 25/07/08. **Robert Pritchard**

▼ East Midlands Trains blue 153 374 and 153 313 (still in North Western Trains blue) pass Barrow-on-Soar with the 15.35 Leicester–Lincoln on 30 July. **Paul Biggs**

▲ Just the rear vehicle of Northern-liveried 155 345 carrys promotional vinyls, as it passes Eastwood, Caldervale with the 09.37 Leeds–Manchester Victoria on 19/05/08. **Gavin Morrison**

▼ Strathclyde PTE-liveried 156 513 passes Magiscroft with the 07.52 Glasgow Queen Street–Cumbernauld on 21/07/08. **Ian Lothian**

▲ 3-car Northern-liveried 158 758 arrives at Preston with the 15.52 York–Blackpool North on 29/06/08. **Robin Ralston**

▼ First Group-liveried 158 736 leaves Helmsdale with the 07.14 Inverness–Wick on 31/05/08. **Adrian Sumner**

▲ A 9-car Class 159/0 formation – 159 002/004/006 – passes Vauxhall on 24/05/08 shortly after departure from London Waterloo with the 09.20 to Plymouth/Bristol Temple Meads. **Alex Dasi-Sutton**

▼ First Great Western "Dynamic Lines"-liveried 166 216 passes Buckland on the North Downs Line with the 11.04 Reading–Redhill on 03/05/08.
Alex Dasi-Sutton

150 010	u	**WM**	A	*LM*	TS	52110	57226	57110
150 011	u	**CI**	A	*LM*	TS	52111	52204	57111
150 012	u	**CI**	A	*LM*	TS	52112	57206	57112
150 013	u	**CI**	A	*LM*	TS	52113	52226	57113
150 014	u	**CI**	A	*LM*	TS	52114	57204	57114
150 015	u	**CI**	A	*LM*	TS	52115	52206	57115
150 016	u	**CI**	A	*LM*	TS	52116	57212	57116
150 017	u	**CI**	A	*LM*	TS	52117	57209	57117
150 018	u	**WM**	A	*LM*	TS	52118	57220	57118
150 019	u	**CI**	A	*LM*	TS	52119	57220	57119
150 101	u	**CI**	A	*LM*	TS	52101	57101	
150 102	u	**CI**	A	*LM*	TS	52102	57102	
150 104	u	**CI**	A	*LM*	TS	52104	57104	
150 106	u	**CI**	A	*LM*	TS	52106	57106	
150 108	u	**CI**	A	*LM*	TS	52108	57108	
150 120	t	**SL**	A	*LO*	WN	52120	57120	Gospel Oak–Barking 2000
150 121	u	**SL**	A	*GW*	PM	52121	57121	
150 122	u	**CI**	A	*LM*	TS	52122	57122	
150 123	t	**SL**	A	*LO*	WN	52123	57123	Willesden TMD
150 124	u	**CI**	A	*LM*	TS	52124	57124	
150 125	u	**CI**	A	*LM*	TS	52125	57125	
150 126	u	**WM**	A	*LM*	TS	52126	57126	
150 127	t	**SL**	A	*GW*	PM	52127	57127	
150 128	t	**SL**	A	*LO*	WN	52128	57128	Bedford-Bamberg 30
150 129	t	**SL**	A	*LO*	WN	52129	57129	MARSTON VALE
150 130	t	**SL**	A	*LO*	WN	52130	57130	Bedford–Bletchley 150
150 131	t	**SL**	A	*LO*	WN	52131	57131	LESLIE CRABBE
150 132		**WM**	A	*LM*	TS	52132	57132	
150 133	c	**NO**	A	*NO*	NH	52133	57133	
150 134	c	**NO**	A	*NO*	NH	52134	57134	
150 135	c	**NO**	A	*NO*	NH	52135	57135	
150 136	c	**NO**	A	*NO*	NH	52136	57136	
150 137	c	**NO**	A	*NO*	NH	52137	57137	
150 138	c	**NO**	A	*NO*	NH	52138	57138	
150 139	c	**NO**	A	*NO*	NH	52139	57139	
150 140	c	**NO**	A	*NO*	NH	52140	57140	
150 141	c	**NO**	A	*NO*	NH	52141	57141	
150 142	c	**NO**	A	*NO*	NH	52142	57142	
150 143	c	**NO**	A	*NO*	NH	52143	57143	
150 144	c	**NO**	A	*NO*	NH	52144	57144	
150 145	c	**NO**	A	*NO*	NH	52145	57145	
150 146	c	**NO**	A	*NO*	NH	52146	57146	
150 147	c	**NO**	A	*NO*	NH	52147	57147	
150 148	c	**NO**	A	*NO*	NH	52148	57148	
150 149	c	**NO**	A	*NO*	NH	52149	57149	
150 150	c	**NO**	A	*NO*	NH	52150	57150	

CLASS 150/2   SPRINTER   BREL YORK

DMSL–DMS.

Construction: Steel.
Engines: One Cummins NT855R5 of 213 kW (285 h.p.) at 2100 r.p.m.
Bogies: BP38 (powered), BT38 (non-powered).
Couplers: BSI.
Dimensions: 19.74 x 2.82 m.
Gangways: Throughout.   **Wheel Arrangement:** 2-B + B-2.
Doors: Twin-leaf sliding.   **Maximum Speed:** 75 m.p.h.
Seating Layout: 3+2 mainly unidirectional seating as built, but most units have now been refurbished with new 2+2 seating (see notes below).
Multiple Working: Within class and with Classes 142, 143, 144, 153, 155, 156, 158, 159, 170 and 172.

DMSL. Lot No. 31017 1986–1987. –/73 1T (c –/62 1TD, p –/60(4) 1T, u –/71 1T), v –/60(8) 1T, w –/60(8) 1T). 37.5 t.
DMS. Lot No. 31018 1986–1987. –/76 (c –/70, p –/56(10) 1W, u –/70), v –/56(15) 2W, w –/56(17) 2W, z –/68.). 36.5 t.

Northern promotional vinyls: 150 271 Rugby League (Northern Rail Cup). 150 272 R&B Festival week, Colne.

Notes:

c 3+2 Chapman seating (former First North Western units).
p Refurbished Arriva Trains Wales units with 2+2 Primarius seating.
v Units refurbished for Valley Lines with 2+2 Chapman seating.
w Units refurbished for First Great Western with 2+2 Chapman seating.

The following units are on short-term sub-lease from Arriva Trains Wales to First Great Western: 150 267/278–281.

150 201	c	**NO**	A	*NO*	NH	52201	57201
150 203	c	**NO**	A	*NO*	NH	52203	57203
150 205	c	**NO**	A	*NO*	NH	52205	57205
150 207	c	**NO**	A	*NO*	NH	52207	57207
150 208	p	**AV**	P	*AW*	CF	52208	57208
150 211	c	**NO**	A	*NO*	NH	52211	57211
150 213	p	**AV**	P	*AW*	CF	52213	57213
150 214	u	**CI**	A	*LM*	TS	52214	57214
150 215	c	**NO**	A	*NO*	NH	52215	57215
150 216	u	**CI**	A	*LM*	TS	52216	57216
150 217	p	**AV**	P	*AW*	CF	52217	57217
150 218	c	**NO**	A	*NO*	NH	52218	57218
150 219	w	**FI**	P	*GW*	EX	52219	57219
150 221	w	**FI**	P	*GW*	EX	52221	57221
150 222	c	**NO**	A	*NO*	NH	52222	57222
150 223	c	**NO**	A	*NO*	NH	52223	57223
150 224	c	**NO**	A	*NO*	NH	52224	57224
150 225	c	**NO**	A	*NO*	NH	52225	57225
150 227	p	**AV**	P	*AW*	CF	52227	57227
150 228		**NO**	P	*NO*	NH	52228	57228

150 229	p	**AV**	P	*AW*	CF	52229	57229
150 230	w	**AV**	P	*AW*	CF	52230	57230
150 231	p	**AV**	P	*AW*	CF	52231	57231
150 232	w	**FI**	P	*GW*	EX	52232	57232
150 233	w	**FI**	P	*GW*	EX	52233	57233
150 234	w	**FI**	P	*GW*	EX	52234	57234
150 235	p	**AV**	P	*AW*	CF	52235	57235
150 236	w	**AV**	P	*AW*	CF	52236	57236
150 237	p	**AV**	P	*AW*	CF	52237	57237
150 238	w	**FI**	P	*GW*	EX	52238	57238
150 239	w	**FI**	P	*GW*	EX	52239	57239
150 240	w	**AV**	P	*AW*	CF	52240	57240
150 241	w	**AV**	P	*AW*	CF	52241	57241
150 242	w	**AV**	P	*AW*	CF	52242	57242
150 243	w	**WZ**	P	*GW*	EX	52243	57243
150 244	w	**FI**	P	*GW*	EX	52244	57244
150 245	p	**AV**	P	*AW*	CF	52245	57245
150 246	w	**FI**	P	*GW*	EX	52246	57246
150 247	w	**FI**	P	*GW*	EX	52247	57247
150 248	w	**FI**	P	*GW*	EX	52248	57248
150 249	w	**FI**	P	*GW*	EX	52249	57249
150 250	p	**AV**	P	*AW*	CF	52250	57250
150 251	w	**AV**	P	*AW*	CF	52251	57251
150 252	p	**AV**	P	*AW*	CF	52252	57252
150 253	w	**AV**	P	*AW*	CF	52253	57253
150 254	w	**AV**	P	*AW*	CF	52254	57254
150 255	p	**AV**	P	*AW*	CF	52255	57255
150 256	p	**AV**	P	*AW*	CF	52256	57256
150 257	p	**AV**	P	*AW*	CF	52257	57257
150 258	p	**AV**	P	*AW*	CF	52258	57258
150 259	p	**AV**	P	*AW*	CF	52259	57259
150 260	p	**AV**	P	*AW*	CF	52260	57260
150 261	w	**FI**	P	*GW*	EX	52261	57261
150 262	p	**AV**	P	*AW*	CF	52262	57262
150 263	w	**WZ**	P	*GW*	EX	52263	57263	The Castles of Cornwall
150 264	p	**AV**	P	*AW*	CF	52264	57264
150 265	w	**WZ**	P	*GW*	EX	52265	57265	The Falmouth Flyer
150 266	w	**FI**	P	*GW*	EX	52266	57266
150 267	v	**AV**	P	*GW*	EX	52267	57267
150 268		**NO**	P	*NO*	NH	52268	57268	Benny Rothman – The Manchester Rambler
150 269		**NO**	P	*NO*	NH	52269	57269
150 270		**NO**	P	*NO*	NH	52270	57270
150 271		**NO**	P	*NO*	NH	52271	57271
150 272		**NO**	P	*NO*	NH	52272	57272
150 273		**NO**	P	*NO*	NH	52273	57273	Driver John Axon G.C.
150 274		**NO**	P	*NO*	NH	52274	57274
150 275		**NO**	P	*NO*	NH	52275	57275
150 276		**NO**	P	*NO*	NH	52276	57276
150 277		**NO**	P	*NO*	NH	52277	57277
150 278	v	**AV**	P	*GW*	EX	52278	57278

150 279	v	**AV**	P	GW	EX	52279	57279
150 280	v	**AV**	P	GW	EX	52280	57280
150 281	v	**AV**	P	GW	EX	52281	57281
150 282	v	**AV**	P	AW	CF	52282	57282
150 283	p	**AV**	P	AW	CF	52283	57283
150 284	p	**AV**	P	AW	CF	52284	57284
150 285	p	**AV**	P	AW	CF	52285	57285

CLASS 153   SUPER SPRINTER   LEYLAND BUS

DMSL. Converted by Hunslet-Barclay, Kilmarnock from Class 155 2-car units.

Construction: Steel underframe, aluminium alloy body and roof. Built from Leyland National bus parts on bogied underframes.
Engine: One Cummins NT855R5 of 213 kW (285 h.p.) at 2100 r.p.m.
Bogies: One P3-10 (powered) and one BT38 (non-powered).
Couplers: BSI.
Dimensions: 23.21 x 2.70 m.
Gangways: Throughout.   **Wheel Arrangement:** 2-B.
Doors: Single-leaf sliding plug.   **Maximum Speed:** 75 m.p.h.
Seating Layout: 2+2 facing/unidirectional.
Multiple Working: Within class and with Classes 142, 143, 144, 150, 155, 156, 158, 159, 170 and 172.

52301–52335. DMSL. Lot No. 31026 1987–1988. Converted under Lot No. 31115 1991–1992. –/72(3) 1T 1W (* –/66(3) 1T 1W, s –/72 1T 1W, t –/72(2) 1T 1W. 41.2 t.
57301–57335. DMSL. Lot No. 31027 1987–1988. Converted under Lot No. 31115 1991–1992. –/72(3) 1T 1W (* –/66(3) 1T 1W. 41.2 t.

Notes: Cars numbered in the 573xx series were renumbered by adding 50 to their original number so that the last two digits correspond with the set number.
* Refurbished East Anglia area units with a bicycle rack.
c Chapman seating.
d Richmond seating.
Units not shown as c or d were reseated using original Class 158 seats.

153 301	d	**NO**	A	NO	NL	52301	
153 302		**DC**	A	EM	NM	52302	
153 303		**AV**	A	AW	CF	52303	
153 304	d	**NO**	A	NO	NL	52304	
153 305	d	**FI**	A	GW	EX	52305	
153 306	cr	**1**	P	EA	NC	52306	
153 307	d	**NO**	A	NO	NL	52307	
153 308		**DC**	A	EM	NM	52308	
153 309	cr	**AR**	P	EA	NC	52309	GERARD FIENNES
153 310	c	**NW**	P	EM	NM	52310	
153 311	c*	**EM**	P	EM	NM	52311	
153 312	s	**AV**	A	AW	CF	52312	
153 313	cs	**NW**	P	EM	NM	52313	
153 314	cr	**1**	P	EA	NC	52314	
153 315	ds	**NO**	A	NO	NL	52315	
153 316	c	**NO**	P	NO	NL	52316	
153 317	d	**NO**	A	NO	NL	52317	

153 318	d	**FI**	A	*GW*	EX	52318
153 319	d	**AV**	A	*EM*	NM	52319
153 320		**AV**	P	*AW*	CF	52320
153 321	c	**EM**	P	*EM*	NM	52321
153 322	cr	**AR**	P	*EA*	NC	52322	BENJAMIN BRITTEN
153 323		**AV**	P	*AW*	CF	52323
153 324	c	**NO**	P	*NO*	NL	52324
153 325	c	**CT**	P	*LM*	TS	52325
153 326	c*	**EM**	P	*EM*	NM	52326
153 327		**AV**	A	*AW*	CF	52327
153 328	d	**NO**	A	*NO*	NL	52328
153 329	c	**FI**	P	*GW*	EX	52329
153 330	cs	**NO**	P	*NO*	NL	52330
153 331	d	**NO**	A	*NO*	NL	52331
153 332	c	**NW**	P	*NO*	NL	52332
153 333	cs	**CT**	P	*LM*	TS	52333
153 334	ct	**CT**	P	*LM*	TS	52334
153 335	cr	**AR**	P	*EA*	NC	52335	MICHAEL PALIN
153 351	d	**NO**	A	*NO*	NL	57351
153 352	d	**NO**	A	*NO*	NL	57352
153 353		**AV**	A	*AW*	CF	57353
153 354	c	**CT**	P	*LM*	TS	57354
153 355		**EM**	A	*EM*	NM	57355
153 356	c	**LM**	P	*LM*	TS	57356
153 357	d	**AV**	A	*EM*	NM	57357
153 358	c	**NW**	P	*NO*	NL	57358
153 359	c	**NW**	P	*NO*	NL	57359
153 360	c	**NW**	P	*NO*	NL	57360
153 361	cs	**FI**	P	*GW*	EX	57361
153 362	d	**AV**	A	*AW*	CF	57362	Dylan Thomas 1914–1953
153 363	cs	**NW**	P	*NO*	NL	57363
153 364	c	**CT**	P	*LM*	TS	57364
153 365	c	**LM**	P	*LM*	TS	57365
153 366	c	**CT**	P	*LM*	TS	57366
153 367	c	**AV**	P	*AW*	CF	57367
153 368	d	**FI**	A	*GW*	EX	57368
153 369	d	**FI**	P	*GW*	EX	57369
153 370	d	**FI**	A	*GW*	EX	57370
153 371	c	**CT**	P	*LM*	TS	57371
153 372	d	**FI**	A	*GW*	EX	57372
153 373	d	**FI**	A	*GW*	EX	57373
153 374		**EM**	A	*EM*	NM	57374
153 375	c	**CT**	P	*LM*	TS	57375
153 376	c	**CT**	P	*EM*	NM	57376
153 377	d	**FI**	A	*GW*	EX	57377
153 378	d	**NO**	A	*NO*	NL	57378
153 379	c	**CT**	P	*EM*	NM	57379
153 380	d	**FI**	A	*GW*	EX	57380
153 381	c	**EM**	P	*EM*	NM	57381
153 382	d	**FI**	A	*GW*	EX	57382
153 383	c	**CT**	P	*EM*	NM	57383

153 384	c	**CT**	P	*EM*	NM	57384
153 385	c	**CT**	P	*EM*	NM	57385

CLASS 155 SUPER SPRINTER LEYLAND BUS

DMSL–DMS.

Construction: Steel underframe, aluminium alloy body and roof. Built from Leyland National bus parts on bogied underframes.
Engines: One Cummins NT855R5 of 213 kW (285 h.p.) at 2100 r.p.m.
Bogies: One P3-10 (powered) and one BT38 (non-powered).
Couplers: BSI.
Dimensions: 23.21 x 2.70 m.

Gangways: Throughout.	**Wheel Arrangement**: 2-B + B-2.
Doors: Single-leaf sliding plug.	**Maximum Speed**: 75 m.p.h.

Seating Layout: 2+2 facing/unidirectional Chapman seating.
Multiple Working: Within class and with Classes 142, 143, 144, 150, 153, 156, 158, 159, 170 and 172.

DMSL. Lot No. 31057 1988. –/76 1TD 1W. 39.0 t.
DMS. Lot No. 31058 1988. –/80. 38.6 t.

Northern promotional vinyls: 155 341–347 Leeds–Bradford–Manchester route (the "Calder Valley").

Note: These units are owned by West Yorkshire PTE, although managed by Porterbrook Leasing Company.

155 341	**NO**	P	*NO*	NL	52341	57341
155 342	**NO**	P	*NO*	NL	52342	57342
155 343	**NO**	P	*NO*	NL	52343	57343
155 344	**NO**	P	*NO*	NL	52344	57344
155 345	**NO**	P	*NO*	NL	52345	57345
155 346	**NO**	P	*NO*	NL	52346	57346
155 347	**NO**	P	*NO*	NL	52347	57347

CLASS 156 SUPER SPRINTER METRO-CAMMELL

DMSL–DMS.

Construction: Steel.
Engines: One Cummins NT855R5 of 213 kW (285 h.p.) at 2100 r.p.m.
Bogies: One P3-10 (powered) and one BT38 (non-powered).
Couplers: BSI.
Dimensions: 23.03 x 2.73 m.

Gangways: Throughout.	**Wheel Arrangement**: 2-B + B-2.
Doors: Single-leaf sliding.	**Maximum Speed**: 75 m.p.h.

Seating Layout: 2+2 facing/unidirectional.
Multiple Working: Within class and with Classes 142, 143, 144, 150, 153, 155, 158, 159, 170 and 172.

DMSL. Lot No. 31028 1988–1989. –/74 (†* –/72, c, t –/70, u –/68) 1TD 1W. 38.6 t.
DMS. Lot No. 31029 1987–1989. –/76 (d –/78, † –/74, t, u –/72) 37.9 t.

Non-standard livery:

156 425, 156 460 & 156 464 Northern experimental. White with two-tone lilac swooshe.

Advertising livery: 156 402 Chapelfield Shopping Centre (white & blue).

Northern promotional vinyls:

156 448 Hadrians Wall Country (Newcastle–Carlisle line).
156 461 Ravenglass & Eskdale Railway.
156 469 Bishop Auckland branch.
156 484 Settle & Carlisle line.
156 490 National Railway Museum.

Notes:

c Chapman seating.
d Richmond seating.

156 401	c*	EM	P	EM	DY	52401	57401
156 402	cr	AL	P	EA	NC	52402	57402
156 403	c*	EM	P	EM	DY	52403	57403
156 404	c*	EM	P	EM	DY	52404	57404
156 405	c*	EM	P	EM	DY	52405	57405
156 406	c*	EM	P	EM	DY	52406	57406
156 407	cr	1	P	EA	NC	52407	57407
156 408	c*	EM	P	EM	DY	52408	57408
156 409	cr	1	P	EA	NC	52409	57409
156 410	c*	EM	P	EM	DY	52410	57410
156 411	c*	EM	P	EM	DY	52411	57411
156 412	cr	CT	P	EA	NC	52412	57412
156 413	c*	EM	P	EM	DY	52413	57413
156 414	c*	EM	P	EM	DY	52414	57414
156 415	c*	EM	P	EM	DY	52415	57415
156 416	cr	1	P	EA	NC	52416	57416
156 417	cr	1	P	EA	NC	52417	57417
156 418	cr	CT	P	EA	NC	52418	57418
156 419	cr	NX	P	EA	NC	52419	57419
156 420	c	FS	P	NO	NH	52420	57420
156 421	c	NO	P	NO	NH	52421	57421
156 422	cr	1	P	EA	NC	52422	57422
156 423	c	FS	P	NO	NH	52423	57423
156 424	c	FS	P	NO	NH	52424	57424
156 425	c	0	P	NO	NH	52425	57425
156 426	c	FB	P	NO	NH	52426	57426
156 427	c	FS	P	NO	NH	52427	57427
156 428	c	FS	P	NO	NH	52428	57428
156 429	c	FB	P	NO	NH	52429	57429
156 430	t	SC	A	SR	CK	52430	57430
156 431	t	SC	A	SR	CK	52431	57431
156 432	t	SC	A	SR	CK	52432	57432
156 433	t	SC	A	SR	CK	52433	57433
156 434	t	SC	A	SR	CK	52434	57434

156 435	t	SC	A	SR	CK	52435	57435
156 436	t	SC	A	SR	CK	52436	57436
156 437	t	SC	A	SR	CK	52437	57437
156 438	d	N0	A	NO	HT	52438	57438
156 439	t	SC	A	SR	CK	52439	57439
156 440	c	FS	P	NO	NH	52440	57440
156 441	c	FS	P	NO	NH	52441	57441
156 442	t	SC	A	SR	CK	52442	57442
156 443	d	N0	A	NO	HT	52443	57443
156 444	d	N0	A	NO	HT	52444	57444
156 445	u	SC	A	SR	CK	52445	57445
156 446	rt	FS	A	SR	CK	52446	57446
156 447	ru	FS	A	SR	CK	52447	57447
156 448	d	N0	A	NO	HT	52448	57448
156 449	u	FS	A	SR	CK	52449	57449
156 450	ru	FS	A	SR	CK	52450	57450
156 451	d	N0	A	NO	HT	52451	57451
156 452	c	FS	P	NO	NH	52452	57452
156 453	ru	FS	A	SR	CK	52453	57453
156 454	d	N0	A	NO	HT	52454	57454
156 455	c	FB	P	NO	NH	52455	57455
156 456	rt	FS	A	SR	CK	52456	57456
156 457	rt	FS	A	SR	CK	52457	57457
156 458	rt	FS	A	SR	CK	52458	57458
156 459	c	FB	P	NO	NH	52459	57459
156 460	c	0	P	NO	NH	52460	57460
156 461	c	N0	P	NO	NH	52461	57461
156 462		FS	A	SR	CK	52462	57462
156 463	d	N0	A	NO	HT	52463	57463
156 464	c	0	P	NO	NH	52464	57464
156 465	ru	FS	A	SR	CK	52465	57465
156 466	c	FS	P	NO	NH	52466	57466
156 467		FS	A	SR	CK	52467	57467
156 468	d	N0	A	NO	NH	52468	57468
156 469	d	N0	A	NO	HT	52469	57469
156 470	d	N0	A	NO	NH	52470	57470
156 471	d	N0	A	NO	NH	52471	57471
156 472	d	N0	A	NO	NH	52472	57472
156 473	d	N0	A	NO	NH	52473	57473
156 474	rt	FS	A	SR	CK	52474	57474
156 475	d	N0	A	NO	HT	52475	57475
156 476	rt	FS	A	SR	CK	52476	57476
156 477	t	FS	A	SR	CK	52477	57477
156 478	rt	FS	A	SR	CK	52478	57478
156 479	d	N0	A	NO	NH	52479	57479
156 480	d	N0	A	NO	HT	52480	57480
156 481	d	N0	A	NO	HT	52481	57481
156 482	d	N0	A	NO	NH	52482	57482
156 483	d	N0	A	NO	NH	52483	57483
156 484	d	N0	A	NO	HT	52484	57484
156 485	ru	FS	A	SR	CK	52485	57485

156 486	d	**NO**	A	*NO*	NH	52486	57486
156 487	d	**NO**	A	*NO*	NH	52487	57487
156 488	d	**NS**	A	*NO*	NH	52488	57488
156 489	d	**NS**	A	*NO*	NH	52489	57489
156 490	d	**NO**	A	*NO*	HT	52490	57490
156 491	d	**NO**	A	*NO*	NH	52491	57491
156 492	rt	**FS**	A	*SR*	CK	52492	57492
156 493	rt	**FS**	A	*SR*	CK	52493	57493
156 494	u	**SC**	A	*SR*	CK	52494	57494
156 495	u	**SC**	A	*SR*	CK	52495	57495
156 496	ru	**FS**	A	*SR*	CK	52496	57496
156 497	d	**NS**	A	*NO*	NH	52497	57497
156 498	d	**NS**	A	*NO*	NH	52498	57498
156 499	rt	**FS**	A	*SR*	CK	52499	57499
156 500	u	**SC**	A	*SR*	CK	52500	57500
156 501		**SC**	A	*SR*	CK	52501	57501
156 502		**SC**	A	*SR*	CK	52502	57502
156 503		**SC**	A	*SR*	CK	52503	57503
156 504		**SC**	A	*SR*	CK	52504	57504
156 505		**SC**	A	*SR*	CK	52505	57505
156 506		**SC**	A	*SR*	CK	52506	57506
156 507		**SC**	A	*SR*	CK	52507	57507
156 508		**SC**	A	*SR*	CK	52508	57508
156 509		**SC**	A	*SR*	CK	52509	57509
156 510		**SC**	A	*SR*	CK	52510	57510
156 511		**SC**	A	*SR*	CK	52511	57511
156 512		**SC**	A	*SR*	CK	52512	57512
156 513		**SC**	A	*SR*	CK	52513	57513
156 514		**SC**	A	*SR*	CK	52514	57514

Names:

156 416   Saint Edmund
156 420   LA' AL RATTY Ravenglass & Eskdale Railway
156 433   The Kilmarnock Edition
156 466   BUXTON Festival

CLASS 158/0   BREL

DMSL(B)–DMSL(A) or DMCL–DMSL or DMSL–MSL–DMSL.

Construction: Welded aluminium.
Engines: 158 701–158 813/158 880–158 890/158 950–158 959: One Cummins NTA855R of 260 kW (350 h.p.) at 1900 r.p.m.
158 815–158 862: One Perkins 2006-TWH of 260 kW (350 h.p.) at 1900 r.p.m.
158 863–158 872: One Cummins NTA855R of 300 kW (400 h.p.) at 2100 r.p.m.
Bogies: One BREL P4 (powered) and one BREL T4 (non-powered) per car.
Couplers: BSI.
Dimensions: 23.21 x 2.70 m.
Gangways: Throughout.   **Wheel Arrangement:** 2-B + B-2.
Doors: Twin-leaf swing plug.   **Maximum Speed:** 90 m.p.h.

Seating Layout: 2+2 facing/unidirectional in all standard and first class except 2+1 in South West Trains first class.
Multiple Working: Within class and with Classes 142, 143, 144, 150, 153, 155, 156, 159, 170 and 172.

DMSL(B). Lot No. 31051 BREL Derby 1989–1992. –/68 1TD 1W. (c, w –/66 1TD 1W, t –/64 1TD 1W). 38.5 t.
MSL. Lot No. 31050 BREL Derby 1991. –/70 1T. 38.5 t.
DMSL(A). Lot No. 31052 BREL Derby 1989–1992. –/70 1T (c, w –/68 1T, * –/64(2) 1T plus cycle stowage area, t –/66 1T). 38.5 t.

The above details refer to the "as built" condition. The following DMSL(B) have now been converted to DMCL as follows:

52701–52736/52738–52741 (First ScotRail). 15/53 1TD 1W (* refurbished sets 14/46(6) 1TD 1W plus cycle stowage area).
52773/774/777. (Former Trans-Pennine Express 2-car units). 16/48 1TD 1W.
52786/52789 (Former South West Trains units). 13/44 1TD 1W.
52799/806/810/812/813 (vehicles from former Trans-Pennine Express 3-car units). 32/32 1TD 1W.

Northern promotional vinyls: 158 784 PTEG: 40 years.
158 787, 158 792–796 Sheffield–Leeds fast service.
158 790 Rugby League (Northern Rail Cup).
158 902, 158 904, 158 905, 158 908 & 158 909 Leeds–Bradford–Manchester route (the "Calder Valley").

Notes:

* Refurbished First ScotRail units fitted with new Grammer seating, additional luggage stacks and cycle stowage areas.
  First ScotRail units (not *) are fitted with Richmond seating.
c Chapman seating.
s Former Trans-Pennine and Central Trains units have been refurbished with new shape seat cushions.
t Arriva Trains Wales and Northern units with some seats removed for additional luggage space.
u Refurbished former South West Trains units with Class 159-style interiors, including first class seating.
w Refurbished First Great Western units. Units 158 745–751 & 158 762 (most formed into 3-car sets) have been fitted with Richmond seating.

The following units are on sub-lease from Northern to First ScotRail until 30 June 2010: 158 782/786/789/867–870.

All First ScotRail 158s are "fitted" for RETB. When a unit arrives at Inverness the cab display unit is clipped on and plugged in. Similarly Arriva Trains Wales units have RETB plugged in at Shrewsbury for working the Cambrian Lines.

158 701	*	**FS**	P	*SR*	IS	52701	57701
158 702	*	**FS**	P	*SR*	IS	52702	57702
158 703	*	**FS**	P	*SR*	IS	52703	57703
158 704	*	**FS**	P	*SR*	IS	52704	57704
158 705	*	**FS**	P	*SR*	IS	52705	57705
158 706	*	**FS**	P	*SR*	IS	52706	57706

158 707	*	**FS**	P	*SR*	IS	52707	57707
158 708	*	**FS**	P	*SR*	IS	52708	57708
158 709	*	**FS**	P	*SR*	IS	52709	57709
158 710	*	**FS**	P	*SR*	IS	52710	57710
158 711	*	**FS**	P	*SR*	IS	52711	57711
158 712	*	**FS**	P	*SR*	IS	52712	57712
158 713	*	**FS**	P	*SR*	IS	52713	57713
158 714	*	**FS**	P	*SR*	IS	52714	57714
158 715	*	**FS**	P	*SR*	IS	52715	57715
158 716	*	**FS**	P	*SR*	IS	52716	57716
158 717	*	**FS**	P	*SR*	IS	52717	57717
158 718	*	**FS**	P	*SR*	IS	52718	57718
158 719	*	**FS**	P	*SR*	IS	52719	57719
158 720	*	**FS**	P	*SR*	IS	52720	57720
158 721	*	**FS**	P	*SR*	IS	52721	57721
158 722	*	**FS**	P	*SR*	IS	52722	57722
158 723	*	**FS**	P	*SR*	IS	52723	57723
158 724	*	**FS**	P	*SR*	IS	52724	57724
158 725	*	**FS**	P	*SR*	IS	52725	57725
158 726		**FS**	P	*SR*	IS	52726	57726
158 727		**FS**	P	*SR*	IS	52727	57727
158 728		**FS**	P	*SR*	HA	52728	57728
158 729		**FS**	P	*SR*	HA	52729	57729
158 730		**FS**	P	*SR*	HA	52730	57730
158 731		**FS**	P	*SR*	HA	52731	57731
158 732		**FS**	P	*SR*	HA	52732	57732
158 733		**FS**	P	*SR*	HA	52733	57733
158 734		**FS**	P	*SR*	HA	52734	57734
158 735		**FS**	P	*SR*	HA	52735	57735
158 736		**FS**	P	*SR*	HA	52736	57736
158 738		**FS**	P	*SR*	HA	52738	57738
158 739		**FS**	P	*SR*	HA	52739	57739
158 740		**FS**	P	*SR*	HA	52740	57740
158 741		**FS**	P	*SR*	HA	52741	57741
158 745	w	**FI**	P	*GW*	PM	52745	57745
158 752		**NO**	P	*NO*	NL	52752	58716	57752
158 753		**NO**	P	*NO*	NL	52753	58710	57753
158 754		**NO**	P	*NO*	NL	52754	58708	57754
158 755		**NO**	P	*NO*	NL	52755	58702	57755
158 756		**NO**	P	*NO*	NL	52756	58712	57756
158 757		**NO**	P	*NO*	NL	52757	58706	57757
158 758		**NO**	P	*NO*	NL	52758	58714	57758
158 759		**NO**	P	*NO*	NL	52759	57759	
158 763	w	**FI**	P	*GW*	PM	52763	57763
158 766	w	**FI**	P	*GW*	PM	52766	57766
158 767	w	**FI**	P	*GW*	PM	52767	57767
158 769	w	**FI**	P	*GW*	PM	52769	57769
158 770	s	**TC**	P	*EM*	NM	52770	57770
158 773	s	**TC**	P	*EM*	NM	52773	57773
158 774	s	**TC**	P	*EM*	NM	52774	57774
158 777	s	**TC**	P	*EM*	NM	52777	57777

158 780	s	**CT**	A	_EM_	NM	52780	57780
158 782	s	**WT**	A	_SR_	HA	52782	57782
158 783		**ST**	A	_EM_	NM	52783	57783
158 784	st	**NO**	A	_NO_	NL	52784	57784
158 785	s	**CT**	A	_EM_	NM	52785	57785
158 786	u	**SR**	A	_SR_	HA	52786	57786
158 787	s	**NO**	A	_NO_	NL	52787	57787
158 788	s	**CT**	A	_EM_	NM	52788	57788
158 789	u	**SR**	A	_SR_	HA	52789	57789
158 790	st	**NO**	A	_NO_	NL	52790	57790
158 791	st	**NO**	A	_NO_	NL	52791	57791
158 792	s	**NO**	A	_NO_	NL	52792	57792
158 793	s	**NO**	A	_NO_	NL	52793	57793
158 794	s	**NO**	A	_NO_	NL	52794	57794
158 795	s	**NO**	A	_NO_	NL	52795	57795
158 796	s	**NO**	A	_NO_	NL	52796	57796
158 797	st	**NO**	A	_NO_	NL	52797	57797
158 798	w	**FI**	P	_GW_	PM	52798	58715	57798
158 799	s	**TC**	P	_EM_	NM	52799	57799
158 806	s	**TC**	P	_EM_	NM	52806	57806
158 810	s	**TC**	P	_EM_	NM	52810	57810
158 812	s	**TC**	P	_EM_	NM	52812	57812
158 813	s	**TC**	P	_EM_	NM	52813	57813
158 815	c	**NO**	A	_NO_	NL	52815	57815
158 816	c	**WT**	A	_NO_	NL	52816	57816
158 817	c	**WT**	A	_NO_	NL	52817	57817
158 818	c	**AV**	A	_AW_	MN	52818	57818
158 819	c	**WB**	A	_AW_	MN	52819	57819
158 820	c	**AV**	A	_AW_	MN	52820	57820
158 821	c	**WB**	A	_AW_	MN	52821	57821
158 822	c	**WB**	A	_AW_	MN	52822	57822
158 823	c	**AV**	A	_AW_	MN	52823	57823
158 824	c	**WB**	A	_AW_	MN	52824	57824
158 825	c	**WB**	A	_AW_	MN	52825	57825
158 826	c	**WB**	A	_AW_	MN	52826	57826
158 827	c	**WB**	A	_AW_	MN	52827	57827
158 828	c	**AV**	A	_AW_	MN	52828	57828
158 829	c	**AV**	A	_AW_	MN	52829	57829
158 830	c	**WB**	A	_AW_	MN	52830	57830
158 831	c	**WB**	A	_AW_	MN	52831	57831
158 832	c	**WB**	A	_AW_	MN	52832	57832
158 833	c	**WB**	A	_AW_	MN	52833	57833
158 834	c	**WB**	A	_AW_	MN	52834	57834
158 835	c	**WB**	A	_AW_	MN	52835	57835
158 836	c	**WB**	A	_AW_	MN	52836	57836
158 837	c	**AV**	A	_AW_	CF	52837	57837
158 838	c	**WB**	A	_AW_	CF	52838	57838
158 839	c	**WB**	A	_AW_	CF	52839	57839
158 840	c	**AV**	A	_AW_	CF	52840	57840
158 841	c	**WB**	A	_AW_	CF	52841	57841
158 842	c	**NO**	A	_NO_	NL	52842	57842

158 843	c	**WB**	A	*NO*	NL	52843	57843
158 844	t	**NO**	A	*NO*	NL	52844	57844
158 845	t	**NO**	A	*NO*	NL	52845	57845
158 846	t	**CT**	A	*EM*	NM	52846	57846
158 847	t	**CT**	A	*EM*	NM	52847	57847
158 848	t	**NO**	A	*NO*	NL	52848	57848
158 849	t	**NO**	A	*NO*	NL	52849	57849
158 850	t	**NO**	A	*NO*	NL	52850	57850
158 851	t	**CT**	A	*NO*	NL	52851	57851
158 852	t	**CT**	A	*EM*	NM	52852	57852
158 853	t	**NO**	A	*NO*	NL	52853	57853
158 854	t	**CT**	A	*EM*	NM	52854	57854
158 855	s	**WE**	A	*NO*	NL	52855	57855
158 856	s	**CT**	A	*EM*	NM	52856	57856
158 857	s	**CT**	A	*EM*	NM	52857	57857
158 858	s	**CT**	A	*EM*	NM	52858	57858
158 859	s	**NO**	A	*NO*	NL	52859	57859
158 860	s	**NO**	A	*NO*	NL	52860	57860
158 861	s	**WT**	A	*NO*	NL	52861	57861
158 862	s	**CT**	A	*EM*	NM	52862	57862
158 863	c	**WT**	A	*EM*	NM	52863	57863
158 864	c	**WT**	A	*EM*	NM	52864	57864
158 865	c	**WT**	A	*EM*	NM	52865	57865
158 866	c	**WT**	A	*EM*	NM	52866	57866
158 867	c	**WT**	A	*SR*	HA	52867	57867
158 868	c	**WT**	A	*SR*	HA	52868	57868
158 869	c	**WT**	A	*SR*	HA	52869	57869
158 870	c	**WT**	A	*SR*	HA	52870	57870
158 871	c	**WT**	A	*NO*	NL	52871	57871
158 872	c	**WT**	A	*NO*	NL	52872	57872

Names:

158 702	BBC Scotland – 75 years
158 707	Far North Line 125th ANNIVERSARY
158 715	Haymarket
158 720	Inverness & Nairn Railway – 150 years
158 784	Barbara Castle
158 796	Fred Trueman Cricketing Legend
158 855	Exmoor Explorer
158 861	Spirit of the South West

Class 158/8. Refurbished South West Trains units. Converted from former Trans-Pennine Express units at Wabtec, Doncaster in 2007. 2+1 seating in first class. Details as Class 158/0 except:

DMCL. Lot No. 31051 BREL Derby 1989–1992. 13/44 1TD 1W. 38.5 t.
DMSL. Lot No. 31052 BREL Derby 1989–1992. –/70 1T. 38.5 t.

158 880	(158 737)	**ST**	P	*SW*	SA	52737	57737
158 881	(158 742)	**ST**	P	*EM*	NM	52742	57742
158 882	(158 743)	**ST**	P	*EM*	NM	52743	57743
158 883	(158 744)	**ST**	P	*SW*	SA	52744	57744

158 884	(158 772)	**ST**	P	*SW*	SA	52772	57772
158 885	(158 775)	**ST**	P	*SW*	SA	52775	57775
158 886	(158 779)	**ST**	P	*SW*	SA	52779	57779
158 887	(158 781)	**ST**	P	*SW*	SA	52781	57781
158 888	(158 802)	**ST**	P	*SW*	SA	52802	57802
158 889	(158 808)	**ST**	P	*SW*	SA	52808	57808
158 890	(158 814)	**ST**	P	*SW*	SA	52814	57814

CLASS 158/9   BREL

DMSL–DMS. Units leased by West Yorkshire PTE. Details as for Class 158/0 except for seating layout and toilets.

DMSL. Lot No. 31051 BREL Derby 1990–1992. –/70 1TD 1W. 38.5 t.
DMS. Lot No. 31052 BREL Derby 1990–1992. –/72 and parcels area. 38.5 t.

Note: These units are leased by West Yorkshire PTE and are managed by HSBC Rail (UK).

158 901	**NO**	H	*NO*	NL	52901	57901	
158 902	**NO**	H	*NO*	NL	52902	57902	
158 903	**NO**	H	*NO*	NL	52903	57903	
158 904	**NO**	H	*NO*	NL	52904	57904	
158 905	**NO**	H	*NO*	NL	52905	57905	
158 906	**NO**	H	*NO*	NL	52906	57906	
158 907	**NO**	H	*NO*	NL	52907	57907	
158 908	**NO**	H	*NO*	NL	52908	57908	
158 909	**NO**	H	*NO*	NL	52909	57909	
158 910	**NO**	H	*NO*	NL	52910	57910	William Wilberforce

CLASS 158/0   BREL

DMSL–DMSL–DMSL. Refurbished units reformed in 2008 for First Great Western. For vehicle details see above.

158 950	w	**FI**	P	*GW*	PM	57751	52761	57761
158 951	w	**FI**	P	*GW*	PM	52751	52764	57764
158 952	w	**FI**	P	*GW*	PM	57748	52762	57762
158 953	w	**FI**	P	*GW*	PM	52748	52750	57750
158 954	w	**FI**	P	*GW*	PM	57747	52760	57760
158 955	w	**FI**	P	*GW*	PM	52747	52765	57765
158 956	w	**FI**	P	*GW*	PM	57749	52768	57768
158 957	w	**FI**	P	*GW*	PM	52749	52771	57771
158 958	w	**FI**	P	*GW*	PM	57746	52776	57776
158 959	w	**FI**	P	*GW*	PM	52746	52778	57778

CLASS 159/0   BREL

DMCL–MSL–DMSL. Built as Class 158. Converted before entering passenger service to Class 159 by Rosyth Dockyard.

Construction: Welded aluminium.
Engines: One Cummins NTA855R of 300 kW (400 h.p.) at 2100 r.p.m.
Bogies: One BREL P4 (powered) and one BREL T4 (non-powered) per car.
Couplers: BSI.
Dimensions: 22.16 x 2.70 m.
Gangways: Throughout.   **Wheel Arrangement:** 2-B + B-2 + B-2.
Doors: Twin-leaf swing plug.   **Maximum Speed:** 90 m.p.h.
Seating Layout: 1: 2+1 facing, 2: 2+2 facing/unidirectional.
Multiple Working: Within class and with Classes 142, 143, 144, 150, 153, 155, 156, 158, 170 and 172.

DMCL. Lot No. 31051 BREL Derby 1992–1993. 24/28 1TD 1W. 38.5 t.
MSL. Lot No. 31050 BREL Derby 1992–1993. –/70(6) 1T. 38.5 t.
DMSL. Lot No. 31052 BREL Derby 1992–1993. –/72 1T. 38.5 t.

159 001	**ST**	P	*SW*	SA	52873	58718	57873	CITY OF EXETER
159 002	**ST**	P	*SW*	SA	52874	58719	57874	CITY OF SALISBURY
159 003	**ST**	P	*SW*	SA	52875	58720	57875	TEMPLECOMBE
159 004	**ST**	P	*SW*	SA	52876	58721	57876	BASINGSTOKE AND DEANE
159 005	**ST**	P	*SW*	SA	52877	58722	57877	
159 006	**ST**	P	*SW*	SA	52878	58723	57878	
159 007	**ST**	P	*SW*	SA	52879	58724	57879	
159 008	**ST**	P	*SW*	SA	52880	58725	57880	
159 009	**ST**	P	*SW*	SA	52881	58726	57881	
159 010	**ST**	P	*SW*	SA	52882	58727	57882	
159 011	**ST**	P	*SW*	SA	52883	58728	57883	
159 012	**ST**	P	*SW*	SA	52884	58729	57884	
159 013	**ST**	P	*SW*	SA	52885	58730	57885	
159 014	**ST**	P	*SW*	SA	52886	58731	57886	
159 015	**ST**	P	*SW*	SA	52887	58732	57887	
159 016	**ST**	P	*SW*	SA	52888	58733	57888	
159 017	**ST**	P	*SW*	SA	52889	58734	57889	
159 018	**ST**	P	*SW*	SA	52890	58735	57890	
159 019	**ST**	P	*SW*	SA	52891	58736	57891	
159 020	**ST**	P	*SW*	SA	52892	58737	57892	
159 021	**ST**	P	*SW*	SA	52893	58738	57893	
159 022	**ST**	P	*SW*	SA	52894	58739	57894	

CLASS 159/1   BREL

DMCL–MSL–DMSL. Units converted from Class 158s at Wabtec, Doncaster in 2006–07 for South West Trains.

Details as Class 158/0 except:
Seating Layout: 1: 2+1 facing, 2: 2+2 facing/unidirectional.

DMCL. Lot No. 31051 BREL Derby 1989–1992. 24/28 1TD 1W. 38.5 t.
MSL. Lot No. 31050 BREL Derby 1989–1992. –/70 1T. 38.5 t.
DMSL. Lot No. 31052 BREL Derby 1989–1992. –/72 1T.38.5 t.

159 101	(158 800)	**ST**	P	*SW*	SA	52800	58717	57800
159 102	(158 803)	**ST**	P	*SW*	SA	52803	58703	57803
159 103	(158 804)	**ST**	P	*SW*	SA	52804	58704	57804
159 104	(158 805)	**ST**	P	*SW*	SA	52805	58705	57805
159 105	(158 807)	**ST**	P	*SW*	SA	52807	58707	57807
159 106	(158 809)	**ST**	P	*SW*	SA	52809	58709	57809
159 107	(158 811)	**ST**	P	*SW*	SA	52811	58711	57811
159 108	(158 801)	**ST**	P	*SW*	SA	52801	58701	57801

CLASS 165/0   NETWORK TURBO   BREL

DMSL–DMS and DMSL–MS–DMS. Chiltern Railways units. Refurbished 2003–2005 with first class seats removed and air conditioning fitted.

Construction: Welded aluminium.
Engines: One Perkins 2006-TWH of 260 kW (350 h.p.) at 1900 r.p.m.
Bogies: BREL P3-17 (powered), BREL T3-17 (non-powered).
Couplers: BSI.
Dimensions: 23.50/23.25 x 2.81 m.
Gangways: Within unit only.   **Wheel Arrangement**: 2-B (+ B-2) + B-2.
Doors: Twin-leaf swing plug.   **Maximum Speed**: 75 m.p.h.
Seating Layout: 2+2/3+2 facing/unidirectional.
Multiple Working: Within class and with Classes 166 and 168.

Fitted with tripcocks for working over London Underground tracks between Harrow-on-the-Hill and Amersham.

58801–58822/58873–58878. DMSL. Lot No. 31087 BREL York 1990. –/82(7) 1T 2W. 40.1 t.
58823–58833. DMSL. Lot No. 31089 BREL York 1991–1992. –/82(7) 1T 2W. 40.1 t.
MS. Lot No. 31090 BREL York 1991–1992. –/106. 37.0 t.
DMS. Lot No. 31088 BREL York 1991–1992. –/94. 39.4 t.

165 001	**CR**	A	*CR*	AL	58801	58834
165 002	**CR**	A	*CR*	AL	58802	58835
165 003	**CR**	A	*CR*	AL	58803	58836
165 004	**CR**	A	*CR*	AL	58804	58837
165 005	**CR**	A	*CR*	AL	58805	58838
165 006	**CR**	A	*CR*	AL	58806	58839
165 007	**CR**	A	*CR*	AL	58807	58840
165 008	**CR**	A	*CR*	AL	58808	58841

165 009	**CR**	A	*CR*	AL	58809		58842
165 010	**CR**	A	*CR*	AL	58810		58843
165 011	**CR**	A	*CR*	AL	58811		58844
165 012	**CR**	A	*CR*	AL	58812		58845
165 013	**CR**	A	*CR*	AL	58813		58846
165 014	**CR**	A	*CR*	AL	58814		58847
165 015	**CR**	A	*CR*	AL	58815		58848
165 016	**CR**	A	*CR*	AL	58816		58849
165 017	**CR**	A	*CR*	AL	58817		58850
165 018	**CR**	A	*CR*	AL	58818		58851
165 019	**CR**	A	*CR*	AL	58819		58852
165 020	**CR**	A	*CR*	AL	58820		58853
165 021	**CR**	A	*CR*	AL	58821		58854
165 022	**CR**	A	*CR*	AL	58822		58855
165 023	**CR**	A	*CR*	AL	58873		58867
165 024	**CR**	A	*CR*	AL	58874		58868
165 025	**CR**	A	*CR*	AL	58875		58869
165 026	**CR**	A	*CR*	AL	58876		58870
165 027	**CR**	A	*CR*	AL	58877		58871
165 028	**CR**	A	*CR*	AL	58878		58872
165 029	**CR**	A	*CR*	AL	58823	55404	58856
165 030	**CR**	A	*CR*	AL	58824	55405	58857
165 031	**CR**	A	*CR*	AL	58825	55406	58858
165 032	**CR**	A	*CR*	AL	58826	55407	58859
165 033	**CR**	A	*CR*	AL	58827	55408	58860
165 034	**CR**	A	*CR*	AL	58828	55409	58861
165 035	**CR**	A	*CR*	AL	58829	55410	58862
165 036	**CR**	A	*CR*	AL	58830	55411	58863
165 037	**CR**	A	*CR*	AL	58831	55412	58864
165 038	**CR**	A	*CR*	AL	58832	55413	58865
165 039	**CR**	A	*CR*	AL	58833	55414	58866

CLASS 165/1   NETWORK TURBO   BREL

First Great Western units. DMCL–MS–DMS or DMCL–DMS.

Construction: Welded aluminium.
Engines: One Perkins 2006-TWH of 260 kW (350 h.p.) at 1900 r.p.m.
Bogies: BREL P3-17 (powered), BREL T3-17 (non-powered).
Couplers: BSI.
Dimensions: 23.50/23.25 x 2.81 m.
Gangways: Within unit only.   **Wheel Arrangement:** 2-B (+ B-2) + B-2.
Doors: Twin-leaf swing plug.   **Maximum Speed:** 90 m.p.h.
Seating Layout: 1: 2+2 facing, 2: 3+2 facing/unidirectional.
Multiple Working: Within class and with Classes 166 and 168.

58953–58969. DMCL. Lot No. 31098 BREL York 1992. 16/66 1T. 38.0 t.
58879–58898. DMCL. Lot No. 31096 BREL York 1992. 16/72 1T. 38.0 t.
MS. Lot No. 31099 BREL 1992. –/106. 37.0 t.
DMS. Lot No. 31097 BREL 1992. –/98. 37.0 t.

165 101	FD	A	GW	RG	58953	55415	58916
165 102	FD	A	GW	RG	58954	55416	58917
165 103	FD	A	GW	RG	58955	55417	58918
165 104	FD	A	GW	RG	58956	55418	58919
165 105	FD	A	GW	RG	58957	55419	58920
165 106	FD	A	GW	RG	58958	55420	58921
165 107	FD	A	GW	RG	58959	55421	58922
165 108	FD	A	GW	RG	58960	55422	58923
165 109	FD	A	GW	RG	58961	55423	58924
165 110	FD	A	GW	RG	58962	55424	58925
165 111	FD	A	GW	RG	58963	55425	58926
165 112	FD	A	GW	RG	58964	55426	58927
165 113	FD	A	GW	RG	58965	55427	58928
165 114	FD	A	GW	RG	58966	55428	58929
165 116	FD	A	GW	RG	58968	55430	58931
165 117	FD	A	GW	RG	58969	55431	58932
165 118	FD	A	GW	RG	58879		58933
165 119	FD	A	GW	RG	58880		58934
165 120	FD	A	GW	RG	58881		58935
165 121	FD	A	GW	RG	58882		58936
165 122	FD	A	GW	RG	58883		58937
165 123	FD	A	GW	RG	58884		58938
165 124	FD	A	GW	RG	58885		58939
165 125	FD	A	GW	RG	58886		58940
165 126	FD	A	GW	RG	58887		58941
165 127	FD	A	GW	RG	58888		58942
165 128	FD	A	GW	RG	58889		58943
165 129	FD	A	GW	RG	58890		58944
165 130	FD	A	GW	RG	58891		58945
165 131	FD	A	GW	RG	58892		58946
165 132	FD	A	GW	RG	58893		58947
165 133	FD	A	GW	RG	58894		58948
165 134	FD	A	GW	RG	58895		58949
165 135	FD	A	GW	RG	58896		58950
165 136	FD	A	GW	RG	58897		58951
165 137	FD	A	GW	RG	58898		58952

CLASS 166   NETWORK EXPRESS TURBO   ABB

DMCL(A)–MS–DMCL(B). First Great Western units, built for Paddington–Oxford/
Newbury services. Air conditioned and with additional luggage space compared
to the Class 165s.

Construction: Welded aluminium.
Engines: One Perkins 2006-TWH of 260 kW (350 h.p.) at 1900 r.p.m.
Bogies: BREL P3-17 (powered), BREL T3-17 (non-powered).
Couplers: BSI.
Dimensions: 23.50 x 2.81 m.
Gangways: Within unit only.   **Wheel Arrangement:** 2-B + B-2 + B-2.
Doors: Twin-leaf swing plug.   **Maximum Speed:** 90 m.p.h.
Seating Layout: 1: 2+2 facing, 2: 2+2/3+2 facing/unidirectional.

Multiple Working: Within class and with Classes 165 and 168.

DMCL (A). Lot No. 31116 ABB York 1992–1993. 16/68 1T. 39.6 t.
MS. Lot No. 31117 ABB York 1992–1993. –/91. 38.0 t.
DMCL (B). Lot No. 31116 ABB York 1992–1993. 16/68 1T. 39.6 t.

166 201	FD	A	GW	RG	58101	58601	58122
166 202	FD	A	GW	RG	58102	58602	58123
166 203	FD	A	GW	RG	58103	58603	58124
166 204	FD	A	GW	RG	58104	58604	58125
166 205	FD	A	GW	RG	58105	58605	58126
166 206	FD	A	GW	RG	58106	58606	58127
166 207	FD	A	GW	RG	58107	58607	58128
166 208	FD	A	GW	RG	58108	58608	58129
166 209	FD	A	GW	RG	58109	58609	58130
166 210	FD	A	GW	RG	58110	58610	58131
166 211	FD	A	GW	RG	58111	58611	58132
166 212	FD	A	GW	RG	58112	58612	58133
166 213	FD	A	GW	RG	58113	58613	58134
166 214	FD	A	GW	RG	58114	58614	58135
166 215	FD	A	GW	RG	58115	58615	58136
166 216	FD	A	GW	RG	58116	58616	58137
166 217	FD	A	GW	RG	58117	58617	58138
166 218	FD	A	GW	RG	58118	58618	58139
166 219	FD	A	GW	RG	58119	58619	58140
166 220	FD	A	GW	RG	58120	58620	58141
166 221	FD	A	GW	RG	58121	58621	58142

CLASS 168   CLUBMAN   ADTRANZ/BOMBARDIER

Air conditioned.

Construction: Welded aluminium bodies with bolt-on steel ends.
Engines: One MTU 6R183TD13H of 315 kW (422 h.p.) at 1900 r.p.m.
Transmission: Hydraulic. Voith T211rzze to ZF final drive.
Bogies: One Adtranz P3–23 and one BREL T3–23 per car.
Couplers: BSI at outer ends, bar within unit.
Dimensions: Class 168/0: 24.10/23.61 x 2.75 m. Others: 23.62/23.61 x 2.75 m.
Gangways: Within unit only.   **Wheel Arrangement:** 2-B (+ B-2 + B-2) + B-2.
Doors: Twin-leaf swing plug.   **Maximum Speed:** 100 m.p.h.
Seating Layout: 2+2 facing/unidirectional.
Multiple Working: Within class and with Classes 165 and 166.

Fitted with tripcocks for working over London Underground tracks between Harrow-on-the-Hill and Amersham.

Class 168/0. Original Design. DMSL(A)–MS–MSL–DMSL(B) or DMSL(A)–MSL–MS–DMSL(B).

58151–58155. DMSL(A). Adtranz Derby 1997–1998. –/57 1TD 1W. 43.7 t.
58651–58655. MSL. Adtranz Derby 1998. –/73 1T. 41.0 t.
58451–58455. MS. Adtranz Derby 1998. –/77. 40.5 t.
58251–58255. DMSL(B). Adtranz Derby 1998. –/68 1T. 43.6 t.

Note: 58451–58455 were numbered 58656–58660 for a time when used in 168 106–168 110.

168 001	**CR**	P	*CR*	AL	58151	58451	58651	58251
168 002	**CR**	P	*CR*	AL	58152	58652	58452	58252
168 003	**CR**	P	*CR*	AL	58153	58653	58453	58253
168 004	**CR**	P	*CR*	AL	58154	58654	58454	58254
168 005	**CR**	P	*CR*	AL	58155	58655	58455	58255

Class 168/1. These units are effectively Class 170s. DMSL(A)–MSL–MS–DMSL(B), DMSL(A)–MS–MSL–DMSL(B) or DMSL(A)–MS–DMSL(B).

58156–58163. DMSL(A). Adtranz Derby 2000. –/57 1TD 2W. 45.2 t.
58456–58460. MS. Bombardier Derby 2002. –/76. 41.8 t.
58756–58757. MSL. Bombardier Derby 2002. –/73 1T. 42.9 t.
58461–58463. MS. Adtranz Derby 2000. –/76. 42.4 t.
58256–58263. DMSL(B). Adtranz Derby 2000. –/69 1T. 45.2 t.

Notes: 58461–58463 have been renumbered from 58661–58663.

168 106	**CR**	P	*CR*	AL	58156	58756	58456	58256
168 107	**CR**	P	*CR*	AL	58157	58457	58757	58257
168 108	**CR**	P	*CR*	AL	58158		58458	58258
168 109	**CR**	P	*CR*	AL	58159		58459	58259
168 110	**CR**	P	*CR*	AL	58160		58460	58260
168 111	**CR**	H	*CR*	AL	58161		58461	58261
168 112	**CR**	H	*CR*	AL	58162		58462	58262
168 113	**CR**	H	*CR*	AL	58163		58463	58263

Class 168/2. These units are effectively Class 170s. DMSL(A)–(MS)–MS–DMSL(B).

58164–58169. DMSL(A). Bombardier Derby 2003–2004. –/57 1TD 2W. 45.4 t.
58365–58367. MS. Bombardier Derby 2006. –/76. 43.3 t.
58464/58468/58469. MS. Bombardier Derby 2003–2004. –/76. 44.0 t.
58465–58467. MS. Bombardier Derby 2006. –/76. 43.3 t.
58264–58269. DMSL(B). Bombardier Derby 2003–2004. –/69 1T. 45.5 t.

168 214	**CR**	P	*CR*	AL	58164		58464	58264
168 215	**CR**	P	*CR*	AL	58165	58365	58465	58265
168 216	**CR**	P	*CR*	AL	58166	58366	58466	58266
168 217	**CR**	P	*CR*	AL	58167	58367	58467	58267
168 218	**CR**	P	*CR*	AL	58168		58468	58268
168 219	**CR**	P	*CR*	AL	58169		58469	58269

CLASS 170 TURBOSTAR ADTRANZ/BOMBARDIER

Various formations. Air conditioned.

Construction: Welded aluminium bodies with bolt-on steel ends.
Engines: One MTU 6R183TD13H of 315 kW (422 h.p.) at 1900 r.p.m.
Transmission: Hydraulic. Voith T211rzze to ZF final drive.
Bogies: One Adtranz P3–23 and one BREL T3–23 per car.
Couplers: BSI at outer ends, bar within later build units.
Dimensions: 23.62/23.61 x 2.75 m.
Gangways: Within unit only.
Doors: Twin-leaf sliding plug.   **Wheel Arrangement:** 2-B (+ B-2) + B-2.
                                            Maximum Speed: 100 m.p.h.
Seating Layout: 1: 2+1 facing/unidirectional (2+2 first class in unrefurbished Class 170/1 end cars). 2: 2+2 facing/unidirectional.
Multiple Working: Within class and with Classes 150, 153, 155, 156, 158, 159 and 172.

Class 170/1. Cross-Country units. Former Midland Mainline sets, these now have their first class declassified but refurbished Cross-Country units (shown *) are having the original first class removed. Lazareni seating (Chapman first class seating in MCRMB). DMCL–MCRMB–DMCL or DMCL–DMCL or *DMSL–MS–DMCL/DMSL–DMCL.

DMCL(A). Adtranz Derby 1998–1999. 12/45 1TD 2W (* DMSL –/59 1TD 2W). 45.0 t.
MCRMB. Adtranz Derby 2001. 21/22 and bar (* MS –/80). 43.0 t.
DMCL(B). Adtranz Derby 1998–1999. 12/52 1T (* DMCL 9/52 1T). 44.8 t

170 101	*	CM	P	XC	TS	50101	55101	79101
170 102	*	XC	P	XC	TS	50102	55102	79102
170 103		CM	P	XC	TS	50103	55103	79103
170 104	*	CM	P	XC	TS	50104	55104	79104
170 105		XC	P	XC	TS	50105	55105	79105
170 106		CM	P	XC	TS	50106	55106	79106
170 107		CM	P	XC	TS	50107	55107	79107
170 108		CM	P	XC	TS	50108	55108	79108
170 109		CM	P	XC	TS	50109	55109	79109
170 110		CM	P	XC	TS	50110	55110	79110
170 111		CM	P	XC	TS	50111		79111
170 112	*	CM	P	XC	TS	50112		79112
170 113	*	CM	P	XC	TS	50113		79113
170 114	*	CM	P	XC	TS	50114		79114
170 115	*	CM	P	XC	TS	50115		79115
170 116		XC	P	XC	TS	50116		79116
170 117	*	CM	P	XC	TS	50117		79117

Class 170/2. National Express East Anglia 3-car units. Chapman seating. DMCL–MSL–DMSL.

DMCL. Adtranz Derby 1999. 7/39 1TD 2W. 45.0 t.
MSL. Adtranz Derby 1999. –/68 1T. Guard's office. 45.3 t.
DMSL. Adtranz Derby 1999. –/66 1T. 43.4 t.

170 201	r	1	P	EA	NC	50201	56201	79201
170 202	r	1	P	EA	NC	50202	56202	79202
170 203	r	1	P	EA	NC	50203	56203	79203
170 204	r	1	P	EA	NC	50204	56204	79204
170 205	r	1	P	EA	NC	50205	56205	79205
170 206	r	1	P	EA	NC	50206	56206	79206
170 207	r	1	P	EA	NC	50207	56207	79207
170 208	r	1	P	EA	NC	50208	56208	79208

Class 170/2. National Express East Anglia 2-car units. Chapman seating. DMSL–DMCL.

DMSL. Bombardier Derby 2002. –/57 1TD 2W. 45.7 t.
DMCL. Bombardier Derby 2002. 9/53 1T. 45.7 t.

170 270	r	1	P	EA	NC	50270	79270
170 271	r	AN	P	EA	NC	50271	79271
170 272	r	AN	P	EA	NC	50272	79272
170 273	r	AN	P	EA	NC	50273	79273

Class 170/3. First Trans-Pennine Express units. Chapman seating.
170 309 renumbered from 170 399. DMCL–DMSL.

50301–50308/50399. DMCL. Adtranz Derby 2000–01. 8/43 1TD 2W. 45.8 t.
79301–79308/79399. DMSL. Adtranz Derby 2000–01. –/65 1T. 45.8 t.

170 301	FT	P	TP	XW	50301	79301
170 302	FT	P	TP	XW	50302	79302
170 303	FT	P	TP	XW	50303	79303
170 304	FT	P	TP	XW	50304	79304
170 305	FT	P	TP	XW	50305	79305
170 306	FT	P	TP	XW	50306	79306
170 307	FT	P	TP	XW	50307	79307
170 308	FT	P	TP	XW	50308	79308
170 309	FT	P	TP	XW	50399	79399

Class 170/3. Units built for Hull Trains. Now in use with First ScotRail and dedicated to Edinburgh/Glasgow–Inverness services. Chapman seating. DMCL–MSLRB–DMSL.

DMCL. Bombardier Derby 2004. 7/41 1TD 2W. 46.5 t.
MSLRB. Bombardier Derby 2004. –/60 1T. Buffet and guard's office 44.7 t.
DMSL. Bombardier Derby 2004. –/71 1T. 46.3 t.

170 393	FS	P	SR	HA	50393	56393	79393
170 394	FS	P	SR	HA	50394	56394	79394
170 395	FS	P	SR	HA	50395	56395	79395
170 396	FS	P	SR	HA	50396	56396	79396

Class 170/3. Refurbished Cross-Country units. Lazareni seating. DMSL–MS–DMCL.

DMSL. Bombardier Derby 2002. –/59 1TD 2W. 45.4 t.
MS. Bombardier Derby 2002. –/80. 43.0 t.
DMCL. Bombardier Derby 2002. 9/52 1T. 45.8 t.

| 170 397 | **XC** | P | *XC* | TS | 50397 | 56397 | 79397 |
| 170 398 | **XC** | P | *XC* | TS | 50398 | 56398 | 79398 |

Class 170/4. First ScotRail "express" units. Chapman seating. DMCL–MS–DMCL.

DMCL(A). Adtranz Derby 1999–2001. 9/43 1TD 2W. 45.2 t.
MS. Adtranz Derby 1999–2001. –/76. 42.5 t.
DMCL(B). Adtranz Derby 1999–2001. 9/49 1T. 45.2 t.

170 401	**FS**	P	*SR*	HA	50401	56401	79401
170 402	**FS**	P	*SR*	HA	50402	56402	79402
170 403	**FS**	P	*SR*	HA	50403	56403	79403
170 404	**FS**	P	*SR*	HA	50404	56404	79404
170 405	**FS**	P	*SR*	HA	50405	56405	79405
170 406	**FS**	P	*SR*	HA	50406	56406	79406
170 407	**FS**	P	*SR*	HA	50407	56407	79407
170 408	**FS**	P	*SR*	HA	50408	56408	79408
170 409	**FS**	P	*SR*	HA	50409	56409	79409
170 410	**FS**	P	*SR*	HA	50410	56410	79410
170 411	**FS**	P	*SR*	HA	50411	56411	79411
170 412	**FS**	P	*SR*	HA	50412	56412	79412
170 413	**FS**	P	*SR*	HA	50413	56413	79413
170 414	**FS**	P	*SR*	HA	50414	56414	79414
170 415	**FS**	P	*SR*	HA	50415	56415	79415
170 416	**FS**	H	*SR*	HA	50416	56416	79416
170 417	**FS**	H	*SR*	HA	50417	56417	79417
170 418	**FS**	H	*SR*	HA	50418	56418	79418
170 419	**FS**	H	*SR*	HA	50419	56419	79419
170 420	**FS**	H	*SR*	HA	50420	56420	79420
170 421	**FS**	H	*SR*	HA	50421	56421	79421
170 422	**FS**	H	*SR*	HA	50422	56422	79422
170 423	**FS**	H	*SR*	HA	50423	56423	79423
170 424	**FS**	H	*SR*	HA	50424	56424	79424

Class 170/4. First ScotRail "express" units. Chapman seating. DMCL–MS–DMCL.

DMCL. Bombardier Derby 2003–2005. 9/43 1TD 2W. 46.8 t.
MS. Bombardier Derby 2003–2005. –/76. 43.7 t.
DMCL. Bombardier Derby 2003–2005. 9/49 1T. 46.5 t.

Note: 170 431 & 170 432 have new uprated engines fitted: MTU 6H1800R83 of 360 kW (483 h.p.) at 1800 r.p.m.

170 425		**FS**	P	*SR*	HA	50425	56425	79425
170 426		**FS**	P	*SR*	HA	50426	56426	79426
170 427		**FS**	P	*SR*	HA	50427	56427	79427
170 428		**FS**	P	*SR*	HA	50428	56428	79428
170 429		**FS**	P	*SR*	HA	50429	56429	79429
170 430		**FS**	P	*SR*	HA	50430	56430	79430
170 431	*	**FS**	P	*SR*	HA	50431	56431	79431
170 432	*	**FS**	P	*SR*	HA	50432	56432	79432
170 433		**FS**	P	*SR*	HA	50433	56433	79433
170 434		**SR**	P	*SR*	HA	50434	56434	79434

Class 170/4. First ScotRail "suburban" units. Chapman seating. DMSL–MS–DMSL.

DMSL. Bombardier Derby 2004–2005. –/55 1TD 2W. 46.3 t.
MS. Bombardier Derby 2004–2005. –/76. 43.4 t.
DMSL. Bombardier Derby 2004–2005. –/67 1T. 46.4 t.

170 450	**FS**	P	*SR*	HA	50450	56450	79450
170 451	**FS**	P	*SR*	HA	50451	56451	79451
170 452	**FS**	P	*SR*	HA	50452	56452	79452
170 453	**FS**	P	*SR*	HA	50453	56453	79453
170 454	**FS**	P	*SR*	HA	50454	56454	79454
170 455	**FS**	P	*SR*	HA	50455	56455	79455
170 456	**FS**	P	*SR*	HA	50456	56456	79456
170 457	**FS**	P	*SR*	HA	50457	56457	79457
170 458	**FS**	P	*SR*	HA	50458	56458	79458
170 459	**FS**	P	*SR*	HA	50459	56459	79459
170 460	**FS**	P	*SR*	HA	50460	56460	79460
170 461	**FS**	P	*SR*	HA	50461	56461	79461

Class 170/4. First ScotRail units. Standard class only units used in the Strathclyde area. Chapman seating. DMSL–MS–DMSL.

50470–50471. DMSL(A). Adtranz Derby 2001. –/55 1TD 2W. 45.1 t.
50472–50478. DMSL(A). Bombardier Derby 2004–2005. –/57 1TD 2W. 46.3 t.
56470–56471. MS. Adtranz Derby 2001. –/76. 42.4 t.
56472–56478. MS. Bombardier Derby 2004–2005. –/76. 43.4 t.
79470–79471. DMSL(B). Adtranz Derby 2001. –/67 1T. 45.1 t.
79472–79478. DMSL(B). Bombardier Derby 2004–2005. –/67 1T. 46.4 t.

170 470	**SC**	P	*SR*	HA	50470	56470	79470
170 471	**SC**	P	*SR*	HA	50471	56471	79471
170 472	**SP**	P	*SR*	HA	50472	56472	79472
170 473	**SP**	P	*SR*	HA	50473	56473	79473
170 474	**SP**	P	*SR*	HA	50474	56474	79474
170 475	**SP**	P	*SR*	HA	50475	56475	79475
170 476	**SP**	P	*SR*	HA	50476	56476	79476
170 477	**SP**	P	*SR*	HA	50477	56477	79477
170 478	**SP**	P	*SR*	HA	50478	56478	79478

Class 170/5. London Midland and Cross-Country 2-car units. Lazareni seating. DMSL–DMSL or *DMSL–DMCL.

DMSL(A). Adtranz Derby 1999–2000. –/55 1TD 2W (* –/59 1TD 2W). 45.8 t.
DMSL(B). Adtranz Derby 1999–2000. –/67 1T (* DMCL 9/52 1T). 45.9 t.

170 501	**LM**	P	*LM*	TS	50501	79501
170 502	**LM**	P	*LM*	TS	50502	79502
170 503	**LM**	P	*LM*	TS	50503	79503
170 504	**LM**	P	*LM*	TS	50504	79504
170 505	**LM**	P	*LM*	TS	50505	79505
170 506	**LM**	P	*LM*	TS	50506	79506
170 507	**LM**	P	*LM*	TS	50507	79507
170 508	**LM**	P	*LM*	TS	50508	79508
170 509	**LM**	P	*LM*	TS	50509	79509

170 510		LM	P	LM	TS	50510	79510
170 511		LM	P	LM	TS	50511	79511
170 512		LM	P	LM	TS	50512	79512
170 513		LM	P	LM	TS	50513	79513
170 514		LM	P	LM	TS	50514	79514
170 515		CT	P	LM	TS	50515	79515
170 516		LM	P	LM	TS	50516	79516
170 517		LM	P	LM	TS	50517	79517
170 518	*	XC	P	XC	TS	50518	79518
170 519	*	XC	P	XC	TS	50519	79519
170 520	*	XC	P	XC	TS	50520	79520
170 521	*	XC	P	XC	TS	50521	79521
170 522	*	XC	P	XC	TS	50522	79522
170 523	*	CT	P	XC	TS	50523	79523

Class 170/6. London Midland and Cross-Country 3-car units. Lazareni seating.
DMSL–MS–DMSL or *DMSL–MS–DMCL.

DMSL(A). Adtranz Derby 2000. –/55 1TD 2W (* –/59 1TD 2W). 45.8 t.
MS. Adtranz Derby 2000. –/74 (* –/80). 42.4 t.
DMSL(B). Adtranz Derby 2000. –/67 1T (* DMCL 9/52). 45.9 t.

170 630		LM	P	LM	TS	50630	56630	79630
170 631		LM	P	LM	TS	50631	56631	79631
170 632		LM	P	LM	TS	50632	56632	79632
170 633		CT	P	LM	TS	50633	56633	79633
170 634		LM	P	LM	TS	50634	56634	79634
170 635		LM	P	LM	TS	50635	56635	79635
170 636	*	XC	P	XC	TS	50636	56636	79636
170 637	*	XC	P	XC	TS	50637	56637	79637
170 638	*	XC	P	XC	TS	50638	56638	79638
170 639	*	CT	P	XC	TS	50639	56639	79639

CLASS 171   TURBOSTAR   BOMBARDIER

DMCL–DMSL or DMCL–MS–MS–DMCL. Southern units. Air conditioned.
Chapman seating.

Construction: Welded aluminium bodies with bolt-on steel ends.
Engines: One MTU 6R183TD13H of 315 kW (422 h.p.) at 1900 r.p.m.
Transmission: Hydraulic. Voith T211rzze to ZF final drive.
Bogies: One Adtranz P3–23 and one BREL T3–23 per car.
Couplers: Dellner 12 at outer ends, bar within unit (Class 171/8s).
Dimensions: 23.62/23.61 x 2.75 m.
Gangways: Within unit only.   **Wheel Arrangement:** 2-B (+ B-2 + B-2) + B-2.
Doors: Twin-leaf swing plug.   **Maximum Speed:** 100 m.p.h.
Seating Layout: 1: 2+1 facing/unidirectional. 2: 2+2 facing/unidirectional.
Multiple Working: Within class and with EMU Classes 375 and 377 in an emergency.

Class 171/7. 2-car units. DMCL–DMSL.

50721–50726. DMCL. Bombardier Derby 2003. 9/43 1TD 2W. 47.6 t.
50727–50729. DMCL. Bombardier Derby 2005. 9/43 1TD 2W. 46.3 t.
50392. DMCL. Bombardier Derby 2003. 9/43 1TD 2W. 46.6 t.
79721–79726. DMSL. Bombardier Derby 2003. –/64 1T. 47.8 t.
79727–79729. DMSL. Bombardier Derby 2005. –/64 1T. 46.2 t.
79392. DMSL. Bombardier Derby 2003. –/64 1T. 46.5 t.

Notes: 171 721–171 726 were built as Class 170s (170 721–170 726), but renumbered as 171s on fitting with Dellner couplers.

171 730 was formerly South West Trains unit 170 392, before transferring to Southern in 2007.

171 721	**SN**	P	*SN*	SU	50721	79721
171 722	**SN**	P	*SN*	SU	50722	79722
171 723	**SN**	P	*SN*	SU	50723	79723
171 724	**SN**	P	*SN*	SU	50724	79724
171 725	**SN**	P	*SN*	SU	50725	79725
171 726	**SN**	P	*SN*	SU	50726	79726
171 727	**SN**	P	*SN*	SU	50727	79727
171 728	**SN**	P	*SN*	SU	50728	79728
171 729	**SN**	P	*SN*	SU	50729	79729
171 730	**SN**	P	*SN*	SU	50392	79392

Class 171/8. 4-car units. DMCL(A)–MS–MS–DMCL(B).

DMCL(A). Bombardier Derby 2004. 9/43 1TD 2W. 46.5 t.
MS. Bombardier Derby 2004. –/74. 43.7 t.
DMCL(B). Bombardier Derby 2004. 9/50 1T. 46.5 t.

171 801	**SN**	P	*SN*	SU	50801	54801	56801	79801
171 802	**SN**	P	*SN*	SU	50802	54802	56802	79802
171 803	**SN**	P	*SN*	SU	50803	54803	56803	79803
171 804	**SN**	P	*SN*	SU	50804	54804	56804	79804
171 805	**SN**	P	*SN*	SU	50805	54805	56805	79805
171 806	**SN**	P	*SN*	SU	50806	54806	56806	79806

CLASS 172   TURBOSTAR   BOMBARDIER

New generation Turbostars on order for London Overground, Chiltern and London Midland. Full details awaited.

Construction: Welded aluminium bodies with bolt-on steel ends.
Engines: One MTU 6H1800R83 of 360 kW (483 h.p.) at 1800 r.p.m.
Transmission: Mechanical. Supplied by ZG, Germany.
Bogies: B5000 type "lightweight" bogies.
Couplers: BSI.
Dimensions: 23.27/23.36 x 2.75 m.
Gangways: London Overground & Chiltern units: Within unit only. London Midland units: Throughout.
Wheel Arrangement:
Doors: Twin-leaf swing plug.
Maximum Speed: 75 m.p.h. (London Midland units 100 m.p.h.)
Seating Layout: 2+2 facing/unidirectional.
Multiple Working: Within class and with Classes 150, 153, 155, 156, 158, 159 and 170.

Class 172/0. London Overground units. DMS–DMS. On order for use on the Gospel Oak–Barking line. Due for delivery late 2009.

59311–59318. DMS. Bombardier Derby 2009.   2W.   . t.
59411–59418. DMS. Bombardier Derby 2009.   . . t.

172 001	A	59311	59411
172 002	A	59312	59412
172 003	A	59313	59413
172 004	A	59314	59414
172 005	A	59315	59415
172 006	A	59316	59416
172 007	A	59317	59417
172 008	A	59318	59418

Class 172/1. Chiltern Railways units. DMSL–DMS. On order. Due for delivery summer 2010.

59111–59114. DMSL. Bombardier Derby 2009–2010.   1TD 2W.   . t.
59211–59214. DMS. Bombardier Derby 2009–2010.   . . t.

172 101	A	59111	59211
172 102	A	59112	59212
172 103	A	59113	59213
172 104	A	59114	59214

Class 172/2. London Midland 2-car units. DMSL–DMS. On order for use on West Midlands suburban services. Due for delivery from spring 2010.

50211–50222. DMSL. Bombardier Derby 2009–2010. –/53(4) 1TD 2W.   . t.
79211–79222. DMS. Bombardier Derby 2009–2010. –/68(3).   . t.

172 211	P	50211	79211
172 212	P	50212	79212
172 213	P	50213	79213

172 214	P	50214	79214
172 215	P	50215	79215
172 216	P	50216	79216
172 217	P	50217	79217
172 218	P	50218	79218
172 219	P	50219	79219
172 220	P	50220	79220
172 221	P	50221	79221
172 222	P	50222	79222

Class 172/3. London Midland 3-car units. DMSL–MS–DMS. On order for use on West Midlands suburban services. Due for delivery from spring 2010.

50331–50345. DMSL. Bombardier Derby 2009–2010. –/53(4) 1TD 2W.   . t.
56331–56345. MS. Bombardier Derby 2009–2010. –/72.   . t.
79331–79345. DMS. Bombardier Derby 2009–2010. –/68(3).   . t.

172 331	P	50331	56331	79331
172 332	P	50332	56332	79332
172 333	P	50333	56333	79333
172 334	P	50334	56334	79334
172 335	P	50335	56335	79335
172 336	P	50336	56336	79336
172 337	P	50337	56337	79337
172 338	P	50338	56338	79338
172 339	P	50339	56339	79339
172 340	P	50340	56340	79340
172 341	P	50341	56341	79341
172 342	P	50342	56342	79342
172 343	P	50343	56343	79343
172 344	P	50344	56344	79344
172 345	P	50345	56345	79345

CLASS 175   CORADIA 1000   ALSTOM

Air conditioned.

Construction: Steel.
Engines: One Cummins N14 of 335 kW (450 h.p.).
Transmission: Hydraulic. Voith T211rzze to ZF Voith final drive.
Bogies: ACR (Alstom FBO) – LTB-MBS1, TB-MB1, MBS1-LTB.
Couplers: Scharfenberg outer ends and bar within unit (Class 175/1).
Dimensions: 23.06/23.93 x 2.80 m.
Gangways: Within unit only.   **Wheel Arrangement:** 2-B (+ B-2) + B-2.
Doors: Single-leaf swing plug.   **Maximum Speed:** 100 m.p.h.
Seating Layout: 2+2 facing/unidirectional.
Multiple Working: Within class and with Class 180.

Class 175/0. DMSL–DMSL. 2-car units.

DMSL(A). Alstom Birmingham 1999–2000. –/54 1TD 2W. 50.7 t.
DMSL(B). Alstom Birmingham 1999–2000. –/64 1T. 50.7 t.

175 001	**AV**	A	*AW*	CH	50701	79701
175 002	**AV**	A	*AW*	CH	50702	79702
175 003	**FS**	A	*AW*	CH	50703	79703
175 004	**AV**	A	*AW*	CH	50704	79704
175 005	**AV**	A	*AW*	CH	50705	79705
175 006	**AV**	A	*AW*	CH	50706	79706
175 007	**AV**	A	*AW*	CH	50707	79707
175 008	**AV**	A	*AW*	CH	50708	79708
175 009	**AV**	A	*AW*	CH	50709	79709
175 010	**AV**	A	*AW*	CH	50710	79710
175 011	**AV**	A	*AW*	CH	50711	79711

Name (carried on one side of each DMSL):

175 003   Eisteddfod Genedlaethol Cymru

Class 175/1. DMSL–MSL–DMSL. 3-car units.

DMSL(A). Alstom Birmingham 1999–2001. –/54 1TD 2W. 50.7 t.
MSL. Alstom Birmingham 1999–2001. –/68 1T. 47.5 t.
DMSL(B). Alstom Birmingham 1999–2001. –/64 1T. 50.7 t.

175 101	**AV**	A	*AW*	CH	50751	56751	79751
175 102	**FS**	A	*AW*	CH	50752	56752	79752
175 103	**FS**	A	*AW*	CH	50753	56753	79753
175 104	**FS**	A	*AW*	CH	50754	56754	79754
175 105	**AV**	A	*AW*	CH	50755	56755	79755
175 106	**FS**	A	*AW*	CH	50756	56756	79756
175 107	**FS**	A	*AW*	CH	50757	56757	79757
175 108	**FS**	A	*AW*	CH	50758	56758	79758
175 109	**FS**	A	*AW*	CH	50759	56759	79759
175 110	**AW**	A	*AW*	CH	50760	56760	79760
175 111	**FS**	A	*AW*	CH	50761	56761	79761
175 112	**FS**	A	*AW*	CH	50762	56762	79762
175 113	**FS**	A	*AW*	CH	50763	56763	79763
175 114	**FS**	A	*AW*	CH	50764	56764	79764
175 115	**FS**	A	*AW*	CH	50765	56765	79765
175 116	**FS**	A	*AW*	CH	50766	56766	79766

Names (carried on one side of each DMSL):

175 103   Mum
175 107   CORONATION ST. ROVERS RETURN
175 111   Brief Encounter
175 112   South Lakes Wild Animal Park SUMATRAN TIGER
175 114   Commonwealth Cruiser
175 116   PETER VL JONES Community Rail Officer – Conwy Valley Line

CLASS 180   ADELANTE   ALSTOM

Air conditioned. This fleet is in a state of flux, with three units in use with First
Great Western at the time of writing (until spring 2009 – 180 102/104/105), two
with First Hull Trains (180 110/111, with 180 113/114 also set to move to this
operator), and a further two at Newton Heath for crew training for Northern
(180 103/106).

Construction: Steel.
Engines: One Cummins QSK19 of 560 kW (750 h.p.) at 2100 r.p.m.
Transmission: Hydraulic. Voith T312br to Voith final drive.
Bogies: ACR (Alstom FBO) – LTB1-MBS2, TB1-MB2, TB1-MB2, TB2-MB2, MBS2-
LTB1.
Couplers: Scharfenberg outer ends, bar within unit.
Dimensions: 23.71/23.03 x 2.80 m.
Gangways: Within unit only.
Wheel Arrangement: 2-B + B-2 + B-2 + B-2 + B-2.
Doors: Single-leaf swing plug.   **Maximum Speed:** 125 m.p.h.
Seating Layout: 1: 2+1 facing/unidirectional, 2: 2+2 facing/unidirectional.
Multiple Working: Within class and with Class 175.

DMSL(A). Alstom Birmingham 2000–2001. –/46 2W 1TD. 51.7 t.
MFL. Alstom Birmingham 2000–2001. 42/– 1T 1W + catering point. 49.6 t.
MSL. Alstom Birmingham 2000–2001. –/68 1T. 49.5 t.
MSLRB. Alstom Birmingham 2000–2001. –/56 1T. 50.3 t.
DMSL(B). Alstom Birmingham 2000–2001. –/56 1T. 51.4 t.

180 101	FG	A		OY	50901	54901	55901	56901	59901
180 102	FG	A	GW	OO	50902	54902	55902	56902	59902
180 103	FG	A		NH	50903	54903	55903	56903	59903
180 104	FG	A	GW	OO	50904	54904	55904	56904	59904
180 105	FG	A	GW	OO	50905	54905	55905	56905	59905
180 106	FG	A		NH	50906	54906	55906	56906	59906
180 107	FG	A		OY	50907	54907	55907	56907	59907
180 108	FG	A		OO	50908	54908	55908	56908	59908
180 109	FG	A		OY	50909	54909	55909	56909	59909
180 110	FG	A	HT	XW	50910	54910	55910	56910	59910
180 111	FG	A	HT	XW	50911	54911	55911	56911	59911
180 112	FG	A		OY	50912	54912	55912	56912	59912
180 113	FG	A		XW	50913	54913	55913	56913	59913
180 114	FG	A		OY	50914	54914	55914	56914	59914

CLASS 185   DESIRO UK   SIEMENS

Air conditioned. Grammer seating.

Construction: Aluminium.
Engines: One Cummins QSK19 of 560 kW (750 h.p.) at 2100 r.p.m.
Transmission: Voith.
Bogies: Siemens.
Couplers: Dellner 12.
Dimensions: 23.76/23.75 x 2.66 m.
Gangways: Within unit only.   **Wheel Arrangement:** 2-B + 2-B + B-2.
Doors: Double-leaf sliding plug.   **Maximum Speed:** 100 m.p.h.
Seating Layout: 1: 2+1 facing/unidirectional, 2: 2+2 facing/unidirectional.
Multiple Working: Within class only.

DMCL. Siemens Uerdingen 2005–2006. 15/18(8) 2W 1TD + catering point. 55.4 t.
MSL. Siemens Uerdingen 2005–2006. –/72 1T. 52.7 t.
DMS. Siemens Uerdingen 2005–2006. –/64(4). 54.9 t.

185 101	FT	H	TP	AK	51101	53101	54101
185 102	FT	H	TP	AK	51102	53102	54102
185 103	FT	H	TP	AK	51103	53103	54103
185 104	FT	H	TP	AK	51104	53104	54104
185 105	FT	H	TP	AK	51105	53105	54105
185 106	FT	H	TP	AK	51106	53106	54106
185 107	FT	H	TP	AK	51107	53107	54107
185 108	FT	H	TP	AK	51108	53108	54108
185 109	FT	H	TP	AK	51109	53109	54109
185 110	FT	H	TP	AK	51110	53110	54110
185 111	FT	H	TP	AK	51111	53111	54111
185 112	FT	H	TP	AK	51112	53112	54112
185 113	FT	H	TP	AK	51113	53113	54113
185 114	FT	H	TP	AK	51114	53114	54114
185 115	FT	H	TP	AK	51115	53115	54115
185 116	FT	H	TP	AK	51116	53116	54116
185 117	FT	H	TP	AK	51117	53117	54117
185 118	FT	H	TP	AK	51118	53118	54118
185 119	FT	H	TP	AK	51119	53119	54119
185 120	FT	H	TP	AK	51120	53120	54120
185 121	FT	H	TP	AK	51121	53121	54121
185 122	FT	H	TP	AK	51122	53122	54122
185 123	FT	H	TP	AK	51123	53123	54123
185 124	FT	H	TP	AK	51124	53124	54124
185 125	FT	H	TP	AK	51125	53125	54125
185 126	FT	H	TP	AK	51126	53126	54126
185 127	FT	H	TP	AK	51127	53127	54127
185 128	FT	H	TP	AK	51128	53128	54128
185 129	FT	H	TP	AK	51129	53129	54129
185 130	FT	H	TP	AK	51130	53130	54130
185 131	FT	H	TP	AK	51131	53131	54131
185 132	FT	H	TP	AK	51132	53132	54132
185 133	FT	H	TP	AK	51133	53133	54133

185 134	FT	H	TP	AK	51134	53134	54134
185 135	FT	H	TP	AK	51135	53135	54135
185 136	FT	H	TP	AK	51136	53136	54136
185 137	FT	H	TP	AK	51137	53137	54137
185 138	FT	H	TP	AK	51138	53138	54138
185 139	FT	H	TP	AK	51139	53139	54139
185 140	FT	H	TP	AK	51140	53140	54140
185 141	FT	H	TP	AK	51141	53141	54141
185 142	FT	H	TP	AK	51142	53142	54142
185 143	FT	H	TP	AK	51143	53143	54143
185 144	FT	H	TP	AK	51144	53144	54144
185 145	FT	H	TP	AK	51145	53145	54145
185 146	FT	H	TP	AK	51146	53146	54146
185 147	FT	H	TP	AK	51147	53147	54147
185 148	FT	H	TP	AK	51148	53148	54148
185 149	FT	H	TP	AK	51149	53149	54149
185 150	FT	H	TP	AK	51150	53150	54150
185 151	FT	H	TP	AK	51151	53151	54151

Chiltern Railways-liveried 165 031 passes Denham Golf Club with the 09.41 Stratford-upon-Avon–London Marylebone on 08/05/08.

Robert Pritchard

▲ One of the original Chiltern Railways Class 168/0s, 168 002, passes Neasden shortly after departure from London Marylebone with the 17.00 to Kidderminster on 08/05/08. **Robert Pritchard**

▼ Cross-Country-liveried 170 521 leaves Gloucester with the 12.45 Cardiff Central–Nottingham on 10/06/08. **Robert Pritchard**

▲ London Midland-liveried 170 507, coupled to a Central 153, pauses at Tame Bridge Parkway with the 14.35 Stafford–Birmingham New Street via Rugeley on 06/05/08. **Cliff Beeton**

▼ Southern-liveried 171 804 is seen near Hurst Green with the 11.08 London Bridge–Uckfield on 02/02/08 **Alex Dasi-Sutton**

▲ Arriva Trains-liveried 175 005 is seen at Tyndall Street, Cardiff with the 08.35 Manchester Piccadilly–Milford Haven on 24/05/08. **Andrew Mist**

▼ First Hull Trains now uses 180s on some services. On 180 111 passes Eaton Lane crossing, south of Retford on 24/05/08 with the 08.02 Hull–London King's Cross. **Andrew Wills**

First Trans-Pennine Express "Dynamic Lines"-liveried 185 145 passes Grindleford in the Hope Valley with the 09.52 Manchester Airport–Cleethorpes South Trans-Pennine service on 09/11/07.

Robert Pritchard

▲ All 220s are now in Cross-Country livery. On 15/06/08 220 001 passes Longport with the 17.36 Birmingham New Street–Manchester Piccadilly.   **Cliff Beeton**

▼ Virgin Trains-liveried 221 107 "Sir Martin Frobisher" passes Llanfairyneubwll as it crosses Anglesey with the 14.15 Holyhead–Crewe on 14/06/08.   **Phil Chilton**

▲ Stagecoach-liveried 222 015 and 222 023, still in Midland Mainline livery at the time of this photograph, pass Cossington with the 08.07 Nottingham–London St. Pancras East Midlands Trains service on 11/08/08. **Paul Biggs**

▼ Network Rail Track Assessment Unit 950 001, which is similar to the Class 150 design, is seen near Wellingborough with a test train from Derby to Bletchley on 06/05/08. **Richard Gennis**

▲ South West Trains-liveried Route Learning Unit 960 012 "John Cameron" (converted from a Class 121) is seen at Clapham Junction sidings on 29/05/08.
William Turvill

▼ Chiltern's Water-Jetting unit 960 301 (converted from a Class 117) passes West Ruislip on leaf clearing duties on 19/10/07. **Alex Dasi-Sutton**

2. DIESEL ELECTRIC UNITS

CLASS 201/202 PRESERVED "HASTINGS" UNIT BR

DMBS–TSL–TSL–TSRB–TSL–DMBS.

Preserved unit made up from two Class 201 short-frame cars and three Class 202 long-frame cars. The "Hastings" units were made with narrow body-profiles for use on the section between Tonbridge and Battle which had tunnels of restricted loading gauge. These tunnels were converted to single track operation in the 1980s thus allowing standard loading gauge stock to be used. The set also contains a Class 411 EMU trailer (not Hastings line gauge) and a Class 422 EMU buffet car.

Construction: Steel.
Engine: One English Electric 4SRKT Mk. 2 of 450 kW (600 h.p.) at 850 r.p.m.
Main Generator: English Electric EE824.
Traction Motors: Two English Electric EE507 mounted on the inner bogie.
Bogies: SR Mk. 4. (Former EMU TSL vehicles have Commonwealth bogies).
Couplers: Drophead buckeye.
Dimensions: 18.40 x 2.50 m (60000), 20.35 x 2.50 m (60116/60118/60529), 18.36 x 2.50 m (60501), 20.35 x 2.82 (69337), 20.30 x 2.82 (70262).
Gangways: Within unit only.
Doors: Manually operated slam.
Brakes: Electro-pneumatic and automatic air.
Maximum Speed: 75 m.p.h.
Seating Layout: 2+2 facing.
Multiple Working: Other ex-BR Southern Region DEMU vehicles.

60000. DMBS. Lot No. 30329 Eastleigh 1957. –/22. 55.0 t.
60116. DMBS (Spare). Lot No. 30395 Eastleigh 1957. –/31. 56.0 t.
60118. DMBS. Lot No. 30395 Eastleigh 1957. –/30. 56.0 t.
60501. TSL. Lot No. 30331 Eastleigh 1957. –/52 2T. 29.5 t.
60529. TSL. Lot No. 30397 Eastleigh 1957. –/60 2T. 30.5 t.
69337. TSRB (ex-Class 422 EMU). Lot No. 30805 York 1970. –/40. 35.0 t.
70262. TSL (ex-Class 411/5 EMU). Lot No. 30455 Eastleigh 1958. –/64 2T. 31.5 t.

201 001	**G**	HD *HD*	SE	60116	60529	70262	69337	60501	60118
Spare	**G**	HD *HD*	SE	60000					

Names:

60000	Hastings
60116	Mountfield
60118	Tunbridge Wells

CLASS 220   VOYAGER   BOMBARDIER

DMS–MSRMB–MS–DMF.

Construction: Steel.
Engine: Cummins QSK19 of 560 kW (750 h.p.) at 1800 r.p.m.
Transmission: Two Alstom Onix 800 three-phase traction motors of 275 kW.
Braking: Rheostatic and electro-pneumatic.
Bogies: Bombardier B5005.
Couplers: Dellner 12 at outer ends, bar within unit.
Dimensions: 23.67/23.00(602xx) x 2.73 m.
Gangways: Within unit only.
Wheel Arrangement: 1A-A1 + 1A-A1 + 1A-A1 + 1A-A1.
Doors: Single-leaf swing plug.
Maximum Speed: 125 m.p.h.
Seating Layout: 1: 2+1 facing/unidirectional, 2: 2+2 mainly unidirectional.
Multiple Working: Within class and with Classes 221 and 222 (in an emergency).
Also can be controlled from Class 57/3 locomotives.

DMS. Bombardier Brugge/Wakefield 2000–2001. –/42 1TD 1W. 48.0 t.
MSRMB. Bombardier Brugge/Wakefield 2000–2001. –/58. 45.0 t.
MS. Bombardier Brugge/Wakefield 2000–2001. –/60 1TD. 44.5 t.
DMF. Bombardier Brugge/Wakefield 2000–2001. 26/– 1TD 1W. 48.1 t.

220 001	XC	HX	XC	CZ	60301	60701	60201	60401
220 002	XC	HX	XC	CZ	60302	60702	60202	60402
220 003	XC	HX	XC	CZ	60303	60703	60203	60403
220 004	XC	HX	XC	CZ	60304	60704	60204	60404
220 005	XC	HX	XC	CZ	60305	60705	60205	60405
220 006	XC	HX	XC	CZ	60306	60706	60206	60406
220 007	XC	HX	XC	CZ	60307	60707	60207	60407
220 008	XC	HX	XC	CZ	60308	60708	60208	60408
220 009	XC	HX	XC	CZ	60309	60709	60209	60409
220 010	XC	HX	XC	CZ	60310	60710	60210	60410
220 011	XC	HX	XC	CZ	60311	60711	60211	60411
220 012	XC	HX	XC	CZ	60312	60712	60212	60412
220 013	XC	HX	XC	CZ	60313	60713	60213	60413
220 014	XC	HX	XC	CZ	60314	60714	60214	60414
220 015	XC	HX	XC	CZ	60315	60715	60215	60415
220 016	XC	HX	XC	CZ	60316	60716	60216	60416
220 017	XC	HX	XC	CZ	60317	60717	60217	60417
220 018	XC	HX	XC	CZ	60318	60718	60218	60418
220 019	XC	HX	XC	CZ	60319	60719	60219	60419
220 020	XC	HX	XC	CZ	60320	60720	60220	60420
220 021	XC	HX	XC	CZ	60321	60721	60221	60421
220 022	XC	HX	XC	CZ	60322	60722	60222	60422
220 023	XC	HX	XC	CZ	60323	60723	60223	60423
220 024	XC	HX	XC	CZ	60324	60724	60224	60424
220 025	XC	HX	XC	CZ	60325	60725	60225	60425
220 026	XC	HX	XC	CZ	60326	60726	60226	60426
220 027	XC	HX	XC	CZ	60327	60727	60227	60427
220 028	XC	HX	XC	CZ	60328	60728	60228	60428

220 029	**XC**	HX *XC*	CZ	60329	60729	60229	60429
220 030	**XC**	HX *XC*	CZ	60330	60730	60230	60430
220 031	**XC**	HX *XC*	CZ	60331	60731	60231	60431
220 032	**XC**	HX *XC*	CZ	60332	60732	60232	60432
220 033	**XC**	HX *XC*	CZ	60333	60733	60233	60433
220 034	**XC**	HX *XC*	CZ	60334	60734	60234	60434

CLASS 221   SUPER VOYAGER   BOMBARDIER

DMS–MSRMB–MS(–MS)–DMF or DMS–MS–MS–MSRMB–DMF (refurbished Virgin West Coast 5-car sets). Built as tilting units but tilt now isolated on Cross-Country units.

Construction: Steel.
Engine: Cummins QSK19 of 560 kW (750 h.p.) at 1800 r.p.m.
Transmission: Two Alstom Onix 800 three-phase traction motors of 275 kW.
Braking: Rheostatic and electro-pneumatic.
Bogies: Bombardier HVP.
Couplers: Dellner 12 at outer ends, bar within unit.
Dimensions: 23.67 x 2.73 m.
Gangways: Within unit only.
Wheel Arrangement: 1A-A1 + 1A-A1 + 1A-A1 (+ 1A-A1) + 1A-A1.
Doors: Single-leaf swing plug.
Maximum Speed: 125 m.p.h.
Seating Layout: 1: 2+1 facing/unidirectional, 2: 2+2 mainly unidirectional.
Multiple Working: Within class and with Classes 220 and 222 (in an emergency). Also can be controlled from Class 57/3 locomotives.

DMS. Bombardier Brugge/Wakefield 2001–2002. –/42 1TD 1W. 56.6 t.
MSRMB. Bombardier Brugge/Wakefield 2001–2002. –/58 (* –/52). 53.1 t.
60951–994. MS. Bombardier Brugge/Wakefield 2001–2002. –/60 1TD (* –/68 1TD). 56.6 t.
60851–890. MS. Bombardier Brugge/Wakefield 2001–2002. –/60 1TD (* –/68 1TD). 53.1 t.
DMF. Bombardier Brugge/Wakefield 2001–2002. 26/– 1TD 1W. 56.6 t.

Notes: * Refurbished Virgin West Coast units. The buffet car is moved to be adjacent to the DF and the seating in this vehicle (2+2 facing) can be used by first or standard class customers depending on demand.

221 114–118 will transfer to Virgin Trains from December 2008.

221 101	*	**VT**	HX *VW*	CZ	60351	60951	60851	60751	60451
221 102		**VT**	HX *VW*	CZ	60352	60752	60952	60852	60452
221 103	*	**VT**	HX *VW*	CZ	60353	60953	60853	60753	60453
221 104	*	**VT**	HX *VW*	CZ	60354	60954	60854	60754	60454
221 105	*	**VT**	HX *VW*	CZ	60355	60955	60855	60755	60455
221 106	*	**VT**	HX *VW*	CZ	60356	60956	60856	60756	60456
221 107		**VT**	HX *VW*	CZ	60357	60757	60957	60857	60457
221 108		**VT**	HX *VW*	CZ	60358	60758	60958	60858	60458
221 109		**VT**	HX *VW*	CZ	60359	60759	60959	60859	60459
221 110		**VT**	HX *VW*	CZ	60360	60760	60960	60860	60460
221 111		**VT**	HX *VW*	CZ	60361	60761	60961	60861	60461

221 112	*	**VT**	HX	*VW*	CZ		60362	60962	60862	60762	60462
221 113		**VT**	HX	*VW*	CZ		60363	60763	60963	60863	60463
221 114		**VT**	HX	*XC*	CZ		60364	60764	60964	60864	60464
221 115		**VT**	HX	*XC*	CZ		60365	60765	60965	60865	60465
221 116		**VT**	HX	*XC*	CZ		60366	60766	60966	60866	60466
221 117		**VT**	HX	*XC*	CZ		60367	60767	60967	60867	60467
221 118		**VT**	HX	*XC*	CZ		60368	60768	60968	60868	60468
221 119		**XC**	HX	*XC*	CZ		60369	60769	60969	60869	60469
221 120		**XC**	HX	*XC*	CZ		60370	60770	60970	60870	60470
221 121		**XC**	HX	*XC*	CZ		60371	60771	60971	60871	60471
221 122		**XC**	HX	*XC*	CZ		60372	60772	60972	60872	60472
221 123		**XC**	HX	*XC*	CZ		60373	60773	60973	60873	60473
221 124		**XC**	HX	*XC*	CZ		60374	60774	60974	60874	60474
221 125		**XC**	HX	*XC*	CZ		60375	60775	60975	60875	60475
221 126		**XC**	HX	*XC*	CZ		60376	60776	60976	60876	60476
221 127		**XC**	HX	*XC*	CZ		60377	60777	60977	60877	60477
221 128		**XC**	HX	*XC*	CZ		60378	60778	60978	60878	60478
221 129		**XC**	HX	*XC*	CZ		60379	60779	60979	60879	60479
221 130		**XC**	HX	*XC*	CZ		60380	60780	60980	60880	60480
221 131		**XC**	HX	*XC*	CZ		60381	60781	60981	60881	60481
221 132		**XC**	HX	*XC*	CZ		60382	60782	60982	60882	60482
221 133		**XC**	HX	*XC*	CZ		60383	60783	60983	60883	60483
221 134		**XC**	HX	*XC*	CZ		60384	60784	60984	60884	60484
221 135		**XC**	HX	*XC*	CZ		60385	60785	60985	60885	60485
221 136		**XC**	HX	*XC*	CZ		60386	60786	60986	60886	60486
221 137		**XC**	HX	*XC*	CZ		60387	60787	60987	60887	60487
221 138		**XC**	HX	*XC*	CZ		60388	60788	60988	60888	60488
221 139		**XC**	HX	*XC*	CZ		60389	60789	60989	60889	60489
221 140		**XC**	HX	*XC*	CZ		60390	60790	60990	60890	60490
221 141		**XC**	HX	*XC*	CZ		60391	60791	60991		60491
221 142		**VT**	HX	*VW*	CZ		60392	60792	60992		60492
221 143		**VT**	HX	*VW*	CZ		60393	60793	60993		60493
221 144		**VT**	HX	*VW*	CZ		60394	60794	60994		60494

Names (carried on MS No. 609xx):

221 101	Louis Bleriot		221 109	Marco Polo
221 102	John Cabot		221 110	James Cook
221 103	Christopher Columbus		221 111	Roald Amundsen
221 104	Sir John Franklin		221 112	Ferdinand Magellan
221 105	William Baffin		221 113	Sir Walter Raleigh
221 106	Willem Barents		221 142	Matthew Flinders
221 107	Sir Martin Frobisher		221 143	Auguste Picard
221 108	Sir Ernest Shackleton		221 144	Prince Madoc

CLASS 222 MERIDIAN/PIONEER BOMBARDIER

Construction: Steel.
Engine: Cummins QSK19 of 560 kW (750 h.p.) at 1800 r.p.m.
Transmission: Two Alstom Onix 800 three-phase traction motors of 275 kW.
Braking: Rheostatic and electro-pneumatic.
Bogies: Bombardier B5005.
Couplers: Dellner at outer ends, bar within unit.
Dimensions: 23.85/23.00 x 2.73 m.
Gangways: Within unit only.   **Wheel Arrangement:** All cars 1A-A1.
Doors: Single-leaf swing plug.   **Maximum Speed:** 125 m.p.h.
Seating Layout: 1: 2+1, 2: 2+2 facing/unidirectional.
Multiple Working: Within class and with Classes 220 and 221 (in an emergency).

222 001–222 006. East Midlands Trains Meridian. 7-car units. DMF–MF–MF–
MSRMB–MS–MS–DMS.

Note: The 7-car units were built as 9-car units, before being reduced to 8-car
sets and then later to 7-car sets to strengthen all 4-car units to 5-cars. 222 007
was built as a 9-car unit but has now been reduced to a 5-car unit.

DMF. Bombardier Brugge 2004–2005. 22/– 1TD 1W. 52.8 t.
MF. Bombardier Brugge 2004–2005. 42/– 1T. 46.8 t.
MSRMB. Bombardier Brugge 2004–2005. –/62. 48.0 t.
MS. Bombardier Brugge 2004–2005. –/68 1T. 47.0 t.
DMS. Bombardier Brugge 2004–2005. –/38 1TD 1W. 49.4 t.

222 001	**ST**	H	*EM*	DY	60241	60445	60341	60621
					60561	60551	60161	
222 002	**ST**	H	*EM*	DY	60242	60346	60342	60622
					60562	60544	60162	
222 003	**ST**	H	*EM*	DY	60243	60446	60343	60623
					60563	60553	60163	
222 004	**ST**	H	*EM*	DY	60244	60345	60344	60624
					60564	60554	60164	
222 005	**ST**	H	*EM*	DY	60245	60347	60443	60625
					60565	60555	60165	
222 006	**ST**	H	*EM*	DY	60246	60447	60441	60626
					60566	60556	60166	

222 007–222 023. East Midlands Trains Meridian. 5-car units. DMF–MC–
MSRMB–MS–DMS. Unit 222 018 was still waiting for the insertion of its 5th car
at the time of writing.

DMF. Bombardier Brugge 2003–2004. 22/– 1TD 1W. 52.8 t.
MC. Bombardier Brugge 2003–2004. 28/22 1T. 48.6 t.
MSRMB. Bombardier Brugge 2003–2004. –/62. 49.6 t.
MS. Bombardier Brugge 2004–2005. –/68 1T. 47.0 t.
DMS. Bombardier Brugge 2003–2004. –/40 1TD 1W. 51.0 t.

222 007	**ST**	H	*EM*	DY	60247	60442	60627	60567	60167
222 008	**ST**	H	*EM*	DY	60248	60918	60628	60545	60168
222 009	**ST**	H	*EM*	DY	60249	60919	60629	60557	60169

222 010	**ST**	H	*EM*	DY	60250	60920	60630	60546	60170
222 011	**ST**	H	*EM*	DY	60251	60921	60631	60531	60171
222 012	**ST**	H	*EM*	DY	60252	60922	60632	60532	60172
222 013	**ST**	H	*EM*	DY	60253	60923	60633	60533	60173
222 014	**ST**	H	*EM*	DY	60254	60924	60634	60534	60174
222 015	**ST**	H	*EM*	DY	60255	60925	60635	60535	60175
222 016	**ST**	H	*EM*	DY	60256	60926	60636	60536	60176
222 017	**ST**	H	*EM*	DY	60257	60927	60637	60537	60177
222 018	**ST**	H	*EM*	DY	60258	60928	60638		60178
222 019	**ST**	H	*EM*	DY	60259	60929	60639	60547	60179
222 020	**ST**	H	*EM*	DY	60260	60930	60640	60543	60180
222 021	**ST**	H	*EM*	DY	60261	60931	60641	60552	60181
222 022	**ST**	H	*EM*	DY	60262	60932	60642	60542	60182
222 023	**ST**	H	*EM*	DY	60263	60933	60643	60541	60183
Spare	**MN**	H		ZC				60444	

222 101–222 104. Hull Trains Pioneer. DMF–MC–MSRMB–DMS.

Note: 222 103 is currently out of traffic (long-term) following accident damage.

DMF. Bombardier Brugge 2005. 22/– 1TD 1W. 52.8 t.
MC. Bombardier Brugge 2005. 11/46 1T. 48.6 t.
MSRMB. Bombardier Brugge 2005. –/62. 49.6 t.
DMS. Bombardier Brugge 2005. –/40 1TD 1W. 51.0 t.

222 101	**HT**	H	*HT*	XW	60271	60571	60681	60191
222 102	**HT**	H	*HT*	XW	60272	60572	60682	60192
222 103	**HT**	H		ZC	60273	60573	60683	60193
222 104	**HT**	H	*HT*	XW	60274	60574	60684	60194

Names (carried on end cars):

222 101	Professor GEORGE GRAY
222 102	Professor STUART PALMER
222 103	Dr JOHN GODBER
222 104	Sir TERRY FARRELL

3. SERVICE DMUS

This section lists vehicles not used for passenger-carrying purposes. Some vehicles are numbered in the special service stock number series. The Plasser type Universal Track Recording Units are now classed as "On Track Plant" vehicles.

CLASS 950   TRACK ASSESSMENT UNIT

DM–DM. Purpose built service unit based on the Class 150/1 design. Gangwayed within unit.

Construction: Steel.
Engine: One Cummins NT-855-RT5 of 213 kW (285 h.p.) at 2100 r.p.m. per power car.
Transmission: Hydraulic. Voith T211r with cardan shafts to Gmeinder GM190 final drive.
Maximum Speed: 75 m.p.h.   **Couplers:** BSI automatic.
Bogies: BP38 (powered), BT38 (non-powered).
Brakes: Electro-pneumatic.   **Dimensions:** 20.06 x 2.82 m.
Doors: Manually operated slam & power operated sliding.
Multiple Working: Classes 142, 143, 144, 150, 153, 155, 156, 158, 159 and 170.

999600. DM. Lot No. 4060 BREL York 1987. 35.0 t.
999601. DM. Lot No. 4061 BREL York 1987. 35.0 t.

950 001	**Y**	NR	*SO*	ZA	999600	999601

CLASS 960   SANDITE & SERVICE UNITS

DMB. Converted from Class 121s. Non gangwayed.

For details see Page 10.

960 011 is a Video Survey Unit.
960 012 is a South West Trains Route Learning Unit.
960 014 is a Chiltern Route Learning Unit that is also hired to other operators.

977723. DMB. Lot No. 30518 Pressed Steel 1960. 38.0 t.
977858–60/66/73. DMB. Lot No. 30518 Pressed Steel 1960. 38.0 t.

960 010	**M**	NR	*CR*	AL	977858	(55024)
960 012	**SD**	SW	*SW*	BM	977860	(55028)
960 013	**N**	NR		AL	977866	(55030)
960 014	**BG**	CR	*CR*	AL	977873	(55022)
960 021	**RO**	NR	*CR*	AL	977723	(55021)

John Cameron

CLASS 960   SANDITE UNIT

DMB. Converted 1991 from Class 122. Non gangwayed.

Construction: Steel.
Engines: Two Leyland 1595 of 112 kW (150 h.p.) at 1800 r.p.m.
Transmission: Mechanical. Cardan shaft and freewheel to a four-speed
epicyclic gearbox with a further cardan shaft to the final drive, each engine
driving the inner axle of one bogie.
Maximum Speed: 70 m.p.h.
Bogies: DD10.   **Couplings:** Screw.
Brakes: Twin pipe vacuum.   **Multiple Working:** Blue Square.
Doors: Manually operated slam.   **Dimensions:** 20.45 x 2.82 m.

975042. DMB. Lot No. 30419 Gloucester 1958. 36.5 t.

960 015   **Y**   NR *CR*   AL   975042   (55019)

CLASS 960   WATER-JETTING UNIT

DMB–MS–DMB. Converted 2003/04 from Class 117. Non gangwayed.

Construction: Steel.
Engines: Two Leyland 1595 of 112 kW (150 h.p.) at 1800 r.p.m.
Transmission: Mechanical. Cardan shaft and freewheel to a four-speed
epicyclic gearbox with a further cardan shaft to the final drive, each engine
driving the inner axle of one bogie.
Maximum Speed: 70 m.p.h.
Bogies: DD10.   **Couplings:** Screw.
Brakes: Twin pipe vacuum.   **Multiple Working:** Blue Square.
Doors: Manually operated slam.   **Dimensions:** 20.45 x 2.84 m.

977987/977988. DMB. Lot No. 30546/30548 Pressed Steel 1959–1960. 36.5 t.
977992. MS. Lot No. 30548 Pressed Steel 1959–1960. 36.5 t.

960 301   **G**   CR *CR*   AL   977987   (51371)   977992 (51375)
                                       977988   (51413)

CLASS 960   DRIVER TRAINING UNIT

Converted from a Class 121.

For details see Page 10.

977968. DMB. Lot No. 30518 Pressed Steel 1960. 38.0 t.

-          **Y**   CS *CS*   RU   977968   (55029)

4. DMUS AWAITING DISPOSAL

The list below comprises vehicles awaiting disposal which are stored on the National Railway network.

IMPORTANT NOTE: DMUs still intact but already at scrapyards, unless specifically there for storage purposes, are not included in this list.

Class 101

Spare	**S**	X	ZA	51231	51500
Spare	**RR**	X	SN	51432	51498

Class 117

Spare	**N**	CR	LM	51350	51383	51408
Spare	**RR**	CR	AL	51411		

Class 122

-	**LH**	X	TE	977941 (55012)

Class 901

Converted from Class 205. For sale.

930 301	**RO**	NR	SE	977939 (60145)	977870 (60660)
				977940 (60149)	

Class 960

Converted from Class 121. 960 302/303 converted for use as Severn Tunnel Emergency Train units, but not actually used as such.

960 011	**RK**	NR	ZA	977859 (55025)
960 302	**Y**	AW	CF	977975 (55027)
960 303	**Y**	AW	CF	977976 (55031)

PLATFORM 5 MAIL ORDER
EUROPEAN HANDBOOKS

The Platform 5 European Railway Handbooks are the most comprehensive guides to the rolling stock of selected European railway administrations available. Each book lists all locomotives and railcars of the country concerned, giving details of number carried and depot allocation, together with a wealth of technical data for each class of vehicle. Each book is A5 size, thread sewn and includes at least 32 pages of colour illustrations. The Benelux and Irish books also contain details of hauled coaching stock.

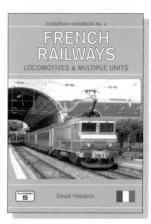

EUROPEAN HANDBOOK No. 4
FRENCH RAILWAYS
LOCOMOTIVES & MULTIPLE UNITS

PLATFORM 5

David Haydock

EUROPEAN HANDBOOKS CURRENTLY AVAILABLE:

No. 1 Benelux Railways (2008) £18.95
No. 2A German Railways Part 1:
  DB Locomotives & Multiple Units (2004) £16.95
No. 2B German Railways Part 2:
  Private Operators, Preserved & Museums (2004) £16.95
No. 3 Austrian Railways (2005) £17.50
No. 4 French Railways (2008) £18.95
No. 6 Italian Railways (2007) £18.50
No. 7 Irish Railways (2008) £12.95

Please add postage: 10% UK, 20% Europe, 30% Rest of World.

Telephone, fax or send your order to the Platform 5 Mail Order Department. See inside back cover of this book for details.

5. CODES

5.1. LIVERY CODES

Code   *Description*

1   "One" (metallic grey with a broad black bodyside stripe. White National Express "interim" stripe as branding).

AL   Advertising/promotional livery (see class heading for details).

AN   Anglia Railways Class 170s (white & turquoise with blue vignette).

AR   Anglia Railways (turquoise blue with a white stripe).

AV   Arriva Trains (turquoise blue with white doors and a cream "swish").

AW   Revised Arriva Trains {Class 175} (turquoise blue with white vignette & two yellow stripes).

BG   BR blue & grey lined out in white.

BI   "Visit Bristol" promotional livery (deep blue with various scenic images).

CI   New Centro {Class 150} (light green with a broad blue lower bodyside band & blue cab end sections).

CM   Revised old Midland Mainline (Midland Mainline teal green with white Central logos).

CR   Chiltern Railways (blue & white with a thin red stripe).

CT   Central Trains (two-tone green with yellow doors. Blue flash and red stripe at vehicle ends).

DC   Scenic lines of Devon & Cornwall promotional livery (black with gold cantrail stripe).

EM   East Midlands Trains {Connect} (blue with red & orange swish at unit ends).

FB   First Group dark blue.

FD   First Great Western "Dynamic Lines" (dark blue with thin multi-coloured lines on lower bodyside).

FG   First Group Inter-City (indigo blue with a white roof & gold, pink & white stripes).

FI   First Great Western "Local Lines" DMU (varying blue with local visitor attractions applied to the lower bodyside).

FS   First Group (indigo blue with pink & white stripes).

FT   First Trans-Pennine Express "Dynamic Lines" (varying blue with thin multi-coloured lines on lower bodyside).

G   BR Southern Region or BR DMU green.

HT   Hull Trains (dark green & silver with two gold stripes).

LH   BR Loadhaul (black with orange cabsides).

LM   London Midland (white/grey & green with broad black stripe around the windows).

M   BR maroon (maroon lined out in straw & black).

MN   Midland Mainline (thin tangerine stripe on the lower bodyside, ocean blue, grey & white).

MY   Merseytravel (yellow & white with a grey stripe).

N   BR Network SouthEast (white & blue with red lower bodyside stripe, grey solebar & cab ends).

NO	Northern (deep blue, lilac & white). Some units have area-specific promotional vinyls (see class headings for details).
NS	Northern Spirit (turquoise blue with a lime green "N").
NW	North Western Trains (blue with gold cantrail stripe & star).
NX	National Express (white with grey ends).
O	Non-standard livery (see class heading for details).
RK	Railtrack (green & blue).
RO	Old Railtrack (orange with white & grey stripes).
RR	Regional Railways (dark blue & grey with light blue & white stripes, three narrow dark blue stripes at vehicle ends).
S	Old Strathclyde PTE (orange & black lined out in white).
SC	Strathclyde PTE (carmine & cream lined out in black & gold).
SD	South West Trains outer suburban {Class 450 style} (deep blue with red doors & orange & red cab sides).
SL	Silverlink (indigo blue with white stripe, green lower body & yellow doors).
SN	Southern (white & dark green with light green semi-circles at one end of each vehicle. Light grey band at solebar level).
SP	Strathclyde PTE {Class 334 style} (carmine & cream, with a turquoise stripe).
SR	ScotRail – Scotland's Railways (dark blue with Scottish Saltire flag & white/light blue flashes).
ST	Stagecoach {long-distance stock} (white & dark blue with dark blue window surrounds and red & orange swishes at unit ends).
TC	Revised Trans-Pennine Express (all over plum).
VT	Virgin Trains silver (silver, with black window surrounds, white cantrail stripe & red roof. Red swept down at unit ends. Black & white striped doors).
WB	Wales & Borders Alphaline (metallic silver with blue doors).
WE	Wessex Trains Alphaline promotional (metallic silver with various images, pink doors).
WM	Network West Midlands (light blue with green lower bodyside stripe and white stripe at cantrail level).
WT	Wessex Trains Alphaline (metallic silver with maroon or pink doors).
WZ	Wessex Trains claret promotional livery with various images.
XC	Cross-Country (two-tone silver with deep crimson ends & pink doors).
Y	Network Rail yellow.
YP	West Yorkshire PTE {DMUs} (red with grey semi-circles).

5.2. OWNER CODES

A	Angel Trains
AW	Arriva Trains Wales
BC	Bridgend County Borough Council/Rhondda Cynon Taff County Borough Council
CC	Cardiff City Council
CR	Chiltern Railways
CS	Colas Rail
ES	Eurailscout GB
H	HSBC Rail (UK)
HD	Hastings Diesels
HX	Halifax Bank of Scotland
NR	Network Rail
P	Porterbrook Leasing Company
RI	Rail Assets Investments
SW	South West Trains
X	Sold for scrap/further use and awaiting collection or owner unknown.

5.3. OPERATOR CODES

AW	Arriva Trains Wales
CA	Carillion Rail
CR	Chiltern Railways
CS	Colas Rail
EA	National Express East Anglia
EM	East Midlands Trains
GW	First Great Western
HD	Hastings Diesels
HT	First Hull Trains
LM	London Midland
LO	London Overground
NO	Northern
SN	Southern
SO	Serco Railtest
SR	First ScotRail
SW	South West Trains
TP	First Trans-Pennine Express
VW	Virgin Trains
XC	Cross-Country

5.4. ALLOCATION & LOCATION CODES

Code	Location	Operator
AK	Ardwick (Manchester)	Siemens
AL	Aylesbury	Chiltern Railways
BM	Bournemouth	South West Trains
CF	Cardiff Canton	Arriva Trains Wales/Pullman Rail
CH	Chester	Alstom
CK	Corkerhill (Glasgow)	First ScotRail
CZ	Central Rivers (Burton)	Bombardier Transportation
DY	Derby Etches Park	East Midlands Trains
EX	Exeter	First Great Western
HA	Haymarket (Edinburgh)	First ScotRail
HT	Heaton (Newcastle)	Northern
IS	Inverness	First ScotRail
LM	Long Marston (Warwickshire)	St. Modwen Properties
MN	Machynlleth	Arriva Trains Wales
NC	Norwich Crown Point	National Express East Anglia
NH	Newton Heath (Manchester)	Northern
NL	Neville Hill (Leeds)	East Midlands Trains/Northern
NM	Nottingham Eastcroft	East Midlands Trains
OO	Old Oak Common HST (London)	First Great Western
OY	Oxley (Wolverhampton)	Alstom
PM	St Philip's Marsh (Bristol)	First Great Western
RG	Reading	First Great Western
RU*	Rugby Rail Plant	Colas Rail
SA	Salisbury	South West Trains
SE	St. Leonards (Hastings)	St. Leonards Railway Engineering
SN*	MoD Shoeburyness	Ministry of Defence
SU	Selhurst (Croydon)	Southern
TE	Thornaby (Middlesbrough)	EWS
TS	Tyseley (Birmingham)	London Midland
WN	Willesden (London)	London Overground
XW	Crofton (Wakefield)	Bombardier Transportation
ZA	RTC Business Park (Derby)	Serco Railtest/Delta Rail
ZB	Doncaster Works	Wabtec
ZC	Crewe Works	Bombardier Transportation
ZD	Derby, Litchurch Lane Works	Bombardier Transportation
ZG	Eastleigh Works	Knights Rail Services/Wabtec
ZH	Springburn Works Glasgow	Railcare
ZI	Ilford Works	Bombardier Transportation
ZJ	Marcroft, Stoke	Turners/Axiom Rail
ZK	Kilmarnock Works	Brush-Barclay
ZN	Wolverton Works	Railcare
ZR	York (Holgate Works)	Network Rail

*= unofficial code.

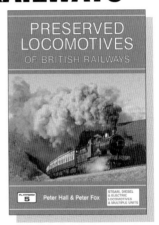